Create
GREETING CARDS
with Glass Painting Techniques

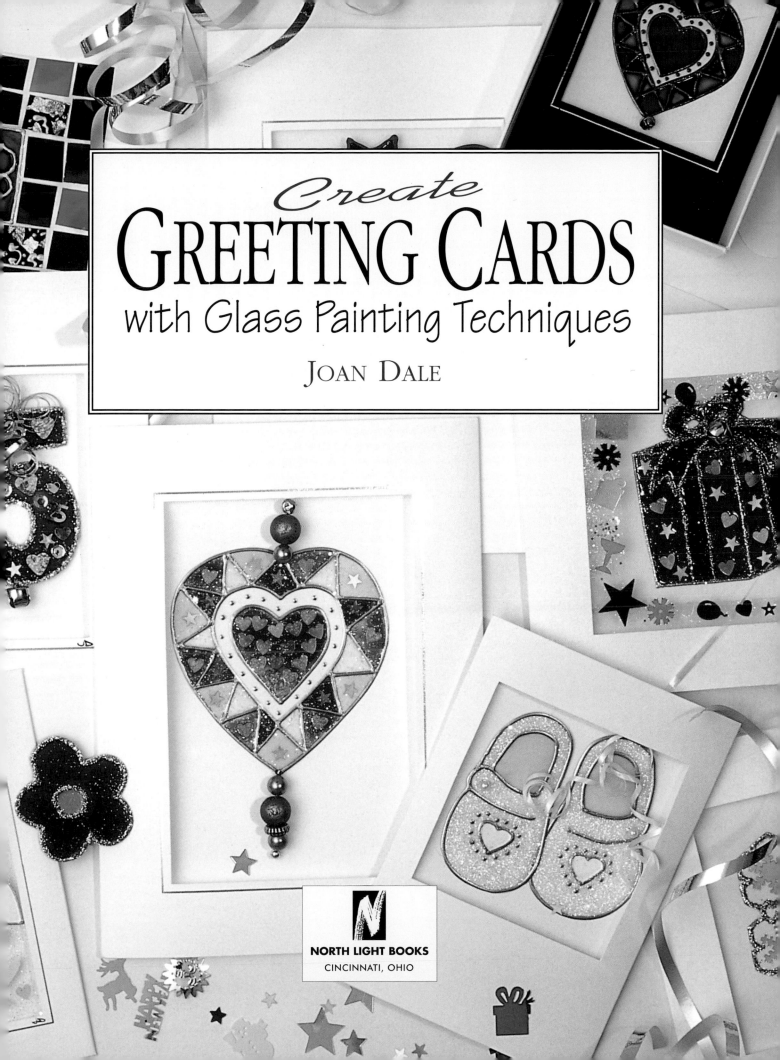

Create

GREETING CARDS

with Glass Painting Techniques

JOAN DALE

NORTH LIGHT BOOKS
CINCINNATI, OHIO

Illustrations © 1999 Joan Dale
Text © 1999 Janet Kirkwood

The moral rights of the illustrator and
the author are hereby asserted.

First published in North America
in 1999 by North Light Books
an imprint of F&W Publications, Inc.
1507 Dana Avenue
Cincinnati, OH 45207
1-800/289-0963

1-58180-007-X

Printed in China

Contents

Introduction 6

Materials 8

Basic Techniques 10

Step-by-Step 12

To My Valentine 23

Birthday Wishes 31

Numerals Templates 38

Happy Christmas 45

Happy New Year 55

Easter 61

Mother's Day 67

Father's Day 73

Bless the Bride 77

Happy Anniversary 83

New Baby 89

Home Sweet Home 93

Good Luck and Bon Voyage 97

Get Well Soon 103

It's Party Time 107

Halloween 113

Blank Cards for Any Occasion 119

Alphabet Templates 124

List of Suppliers 128

Introduction

Nothing shows you care about someone more than giving them something that you have spent time and trouble making yourself. The greeting cards included in this book all use glass-painting techniques.

Double Sequin and Confetti Heart, page 26

When placed near a light source (a window or a lamp) glass painted cards also have a magical 'stained glass' effect which other cards lack.

There are suggestions for every occasion, ranging from Valentine cards to Easter greetings, from birthdays and Christmas to party invitations, and you will be certain to find a suitable card to help celebrate a special event.

The technique is surprisingly simple, and once you have practised tracing the motifs and images of your choice onto acetate and then using the special paints to complete the designs, you will quickly find that you are able to produce stylish cards that will

surprise and please the recipients. This is, too, a craft that is suitable for children, who will enjoy using the colourful paints to produce a wide variety of decorative cards.

All the materials and techniques you will need to complete the cards are described in the first sections, and you will find helpful step-by-step illustrations to guide you through the initial stages. Do read these pages before you begin work: the same techniques are used in all the cards. Note, too, that although dimensions are given in

Christmas Tree, page 46

both imperial and metric versions, you should use one system or the other. Do not try to combine them because conversions can never be absolutely accurate.

The paints, outliner and acetate on which the designs are painted are readily available from stationers, craft shops and department stores and are not expensive. You will probably already have other materials and equipment in your workbox and desk drawer.

Some of the cards are decorated with beads, ribbons and bells. Again, these items

Father's Day Yacht, page 74

are widely available. If you have difficulty obtaining materials, consult the suppliers who are listed on page 128, or look through the advertisements in your favourite craft magazine.

Each of the design projects in this book is accompanied by a template. For your first cards, we would recommend that you either trace from the book or, if you have access to a photocopier, copy the template of your

Wedding Bells, page 80

choice. They are shown here at the most appropriate size for the list of materials included for each card, but they can, of course, be enlarged or reduced as you wish. As you gain experience, you may want to adapt or combine templates or even draw your own. There are also some letters and numerals, which you can copy and adapt to create personal cards for special friends and occasions.

If you follow the simple guidelines on the following pages, you will very soon be creating unusual and eye-catching cards for every date in your diary.

Materials

This section outlines the materials and equipment you will need to complete the projects in this book. You will find everything in your local stationer's, craft shop or department store, but if you have any difficulty in obtaining materials, consult the suppliers listed on page 128.

CARDS

An assortment of double-fold greeting cards, both with and without apertures, is used for the projects illustrated in this book. They are available with or without silver and gold borders. Envelopes are usually provided with the greeting card, but shallow boxes offer better protection in the mail for heavily decorated or for three-dimensional cards.

ACETATE

The transparent sheets of film are also known as OHP and photocopy film. The paint is applied to the surface of the acetate, and this creates a translucent glass painted effect.

TEMPLATE

The template acts as a guide for the outline of the design. Each project is accompanied by a template, shown actual size, which may be photocopied (and reduced or enlarged) or traced from the page.

OUTLINER

An imitation 'lead' is applied to the surface of the acetate to outline the design. When it is dry, it becomes hard and acts as a barrier between paints when they are applied to the acetate. The outliner takes about 2 hours to dry.

BRUSHES

Synthetic watercolour brushes are ideal. Round sizes 2 and 3 are most useful.

PAINT

Both spirit-based and water-based paints have been used throughout this book. If you prefer, the projects can be painted entirely with water-based colours, or entirely with spirit-based colours. The choice is yours. You may also wish to change some of the colours shown in the designs. Ensure there is proper ventilation in your workroom when using spirit-based paints. When children are painting the projects always give them water-based paints to use.

THINNER

Use White spirit, or the manufacturer's recommended thinner, to dilute spirit-based paints, and for cleaning brushes. Do not allow children to handle these chemicals.

VARNISH

The clear liquid is used as a gloss finish and also acts as an adhesive for decorative finishes. Allowabout 24 hours for varnishes to dry.

GLITTER

You should use a good quality, fine glitter, such as Lazer glitter, when you want to add sparkle to your designs. Spirit-based wet paint will sometime bleed into the glitter. The use of water-based paints will help to prevent bleeding.

DECORATION

A wide range of products is available for adding creative decoration to your cards. Build up an extensive stock so that you have a good selection of decorative finishes for your designs.

They can include tinsel, paper ribbon in various widths and colours, shells, sand, bells, ribbons, bows, tassels, wool and yarns. Look out for decorative sequins, beads and jewels which will add to the uniqueness of your work. Always use the best possible sequins for the projects, as they will not bleed when they are applied to the wet surface of the paint or varnish.

Basic Techniques

Making the cards described in this book is not difficult. Children will also enjoy creating their own designs to give to their friends. The basic techniques are explained here, and other techniques are shown in step-by-step form on pages 12-21

OUTLINING A DESIGN

The acetate

When you are working on a mobile or free-standing design, the acetate is *not* cut to the size required for that design until the design is complete, with outliner, paint and decoration in place. It may be left as a sheet or cut large enough for the design with extra all round, so that the piece can be taped to a flat surface without the tape obstructing the area of the design.

For designs that are stuck to the inside edges of the card aperture, the acetate is cut 15mm (⅝in) larger all round than the aperture. This allows for the acetate to be stuck down without obscuring the design.

The template

Photocopy the template or trace the motif provided with the design on to a clean piece of tracing paper.

Secure the copy of the template to a clean, flat surface with tape. Lay the acetate over the template and hold it in place with tape.

Applying outliner

When you are working on a design, resting your hand on a piece of clean paper will avoid marking the surface of the acetate. Follow the outline of the design from the template. Apply the outliner as smoothly as possible by placing the nozzle close to the surface of the acetate and laying the outliner on the acetate.

To obtain a glitter outline to the design, sprinkle glitter over the wet outliner. Shake off the excess glitter and allow the outliner to dry so that the glitter adheres to it.

CUTTING OUT MOBILE OR FREE-STANDING DESIGNS

After the surface of the design is complete and completely dry, use a pair of sharp scissors to cut around the outer edge of the shape, cutting close to the outliner but not through it. If necessary, cut out any inner areas of the design with a craft knife or scalpel. Always take care and do not allow children to handle sharp knives and scissors.

PAINTING THE DESIGN

Always make sure that the paintbrush is cleaned after every use. Clean it thoroughly with white spirit (or thinner) when you have used spirit-

based paints and with water when you have used water-based paints. Dry the bristles with a paper towel or tissue. It is helpful to have several different size brushes to hand, smaller ones for detail and bigger ones for larger areas.

Apply the paint smoothly to the acetate, making sure that the paint goes up to the outliner but not over it. If you leave gaps in the paint, or between the paint and the outliner, unwanted light will shine through.

Designs that do not include an outliner – for example, the three-dimensional Christmas tree – are completed differently. Cut the sheet of acetate so that it is large enough to incorporate the template. Apply the paint so that it covers the entire surface of the acetate, and decorate it if necessary. When the paint is dry, lay the template over the painted surface, thus preventing fingerprints from marking the surface, and cut out the acetate shape following the outline of the design.

If a design incorporates more than one colour and does not include an outliner to separate the colours – for example, Palm Beach – masking tape is used to tape off the section that is not being painted. For this particular design, the top section is painted first. Before you begin to paint, therefore, tape this section off at the lower edge. Apply the paint, and when the section is complete, remove the tape and tape off the section below it. Continue in this way until the design is finished.

DECORATING THE DESIGN

When you are using glitter, sequins, beads or jewels to decorate the surface of a design, they are placed on the wet surface of the paint or varnish with tweezers. As the paint or varnish dries, the decoration adheres to the surface.

If the paint has dried before the decoration has been applied, use a paintbrush to apply a small amount of varnish so that the decoration will stick exactly where you want it.

When applying outliner to a painted surface the paint must be absolutely dry. As the outliner dries it will then adhere to the painted surface.

When you are using other forms of decoration or materials for construction – for example, ribbons, bows, magnets, wool, pipe cleaners or wooden skewers – use a glue gun or strong glue to stick these in place. For other materials – such as craft wire or invisible thread – small, good quality stickers can be used to hold them in place at the back of the card aperture.

FINAL ASSEMBLY

The method used to attach the design to the card will depend on whether you are making a mobile design or a fixed design. A mobile design has a length of invisible thread attached to it so that the mobile will hang in the card aperture. The loose end of the thread is held on the inside top edge of the aperture with a small sticker.

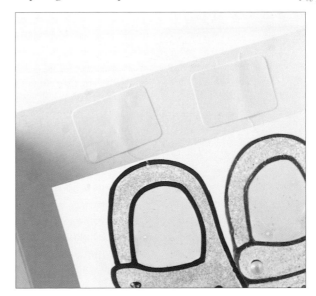

A fixed design is cut so that the acetate is larger than the card aperture. This enables the design to be stuck to the inside edges of the aperture.

Step-by-Step

Tracing numbers is a good way of improving your skills in controlling the tube of outliner, and you will soon become confident enough to master these and the alphabet. Templates for numbers 0 to 9 are on pages 38–9, and alphabet templates are on pages 124–7. There are many sources of alternative numbers and alphabets, and you may wish to copy or adapt them with your own decorations. Bookshops and craft stores usually have a good range of copyright-free designs, or you may even have a selection on your home computer.

2. Number 2 calls for a little more skill in following the rounded contour of the number. If you do make a mistake, wipe it off at once with a paper towel. If the outliner has dried it can be scraped off with a sharp craft knife.

1. Number 1 is a simple exercise in drawing straight lines and learning to avoid blobs where the lines meet. Attach the template tracing (or a photocopy) to a flat surface and tape the acetate firmly in place over the number. Follow the outline of the design using a grey outliner. Apply the outliner as smoothly as possible by placing the nozzle close to the acetate.

3. Paint should be applied carefully but with a well-loaded brush. Turn the acetate if necessary so that you can clearly see the section you are painting. Do not allow the colour to run over the outline.

4. For best results the paint should be applied generously, and this will produce a rich, even colour, which will provide a good base for further decoration.

5. Before the paint is dry, lightly but evenly sprinkle glitter over the whole number. Use a fine glitter if possible. My favourite is Lazer crystal glitter, but do not be afraid to experiment with other types.

6. After applying the glitter, use a pair of tweezers to position the various gold and silver stars, sun and moon. Allow the paint to dry for about 24 hours.

7. When the paint is completely dry the card may then be finished and assembled. Using sharp scissors, carefully cut around the 7 shape. Thread a needle with invisible thread, sew the bell to the foot of the number and secure with a knot. In a similar way, attach a length of thread to the centre of the top edge. Place the end of the thread inside the top edge of the aperture of the card and secure with a self-adhesive sticker.

Painting an outlined design

*Most of the designs in this book involve outlining
the different colour areas of the design and then applying
glass paint inside the outlining.
The double heart shown below is featured on page 27,
where materials and colours are listed.*

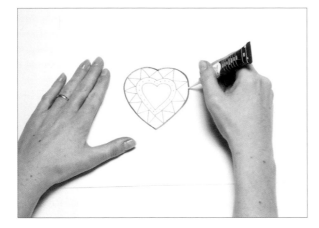

1. Attach the template tracing (or photocopy) to a flat surface and tape the acetate firmly in place over the design. Follow the outline of the design using a grey outliner.

2. Continue following the outline of the design, making sure that you do not create any large blobs when you join two lines together.

3. Complete the outlining of the design and apply evenly spaced dots in the narrow border between the heart shapes. Allow at least 2 hours for the outliner to dry before applying any colours.

4. Start painting at the centre of the design and apply paint generously to obtain a rich colour. The paint should run up to, but not over, the outliner. Paint the outer heart shape by starting at the top and working in a clockwise direction.

5. Continue to fill in the colour sections until the design is complete. When you apply different colours to the design remember to clean the brush thoroughly after each colour application. When all areas are complete, leave to dry for about 24 hours.

6. When the paint is completely dry, the card is ready for finishing and assembly. Carefully cut around the heart shape with a sharp pair of scissors. Using a needle and invisible thread, attach the bell to the lower point of the heart and secure with a knot, then attach a length of thread to the centre top edge. Finally, place the end of the thread inside the top edge of the aperture and secure with a small sticker.

Painting a design that does not have outlined edges

The step-by-step example below features the Palm Beach design (see pages 101–2 for materials) and is painted in a different way from the two previous step-by-step examples. No outliner is used to divide the areas of the design but an 'acetate pen' (OHP pen) is used for drawing the palm tree and yacht.

2. With sharp scissors, carefully cut out the palm tree and yacht shapes following the lines drawn with the acetate pen.

1. Attach the palm tree and yacht template tracing (or photocopy) to your work surface and tape the acetate firmly in place over it. Using the acetate (OHP) pen, trace the palm tree and yacht shapes. Allow to dry then paint the leaves Emerald Green. Do not worry if you go over the lines slightly. Paint the trunk Brown and the yacht Emerald Green. Leave to dry for about 24 hours.

3. Use tape to secure an oblong piece of acetate over the background template. Stick a strip of masking tape across the acetate below the first line on the template. Paint the top section with Deep Blue. While the paint is wet, carefully peel off the masking tape.

4. Place a second strip of masking tape below the second line of the template. Paint the area above this Turquoise Blue and allow the paint to blend gently with the Deep Blue above. This forms the horizon. Use the wooden handle of the brush to draw (scratch) waves in the wet Turquoise Blue. Carefully remove the masking tape. Place a third strip of masking tape below the third line of the template. Paint Cyan above this. While this is still wet, peel off the tape and paint the bottom section White Allow it to blend gently with the Cyan.

5. While the White is still wet, sprinkle it with fine sand (or gold glitter if sand is not available). Take care to sprinkle only the White section. Using tweezers, carefully position tiny sea shells on the still wet paint. Leave to dry for about 24 hours.

6. When the background is completely dry, paint clear varnish on the palm tree and yacht and stick to the reverse side of the acetate. Place the tree at the edge of the beach and the yacht on the horizon. Leave to dry. Apply glue to the inside edge of the aperture and, with the correct side of the design facing outwards, position the acetate and stick down.

Colourful Daisies

The instructions given below are for the design on pages 101–2, where the materials are listed. The actual painting is very straightforward but the fun part is creating the three-dimensional effect using, of all things, pipe cleaners.

1. Tape the acetate in position over the daisy template and carefully follow the outline with silver outliner. Make four more daisy outlines and then one flowerpot outline.

2. While the outliner is still wet, sprinkle it with Lazer silver glitter. Shake off the excess glitter and leave to dry for about 2 hours.

3. When the outliner is dry, paint the outer area of the flower petals Coral, Ruby, Fuchsia Pink, Garnet and Saffron.

4. Paint the flowerpot Lapis Blue. Leave to dry for 48 hours.

5. With a well-loaded brush, carefully paint the centres of the flowers Emerald, Parma, Azurite, Ming Blue and Fuchsia Pink. Leave to dry for 48 hours.

6. When the paint is dry, use sharp scissors to cut around the flower and pot shapes. Cut a 12cm (4³⁄₄in) length of pipe cleaner for each flower.

7. With a glue gun or strong glue apply a spot of glue to the back of each flower. Stick the end of the pipe cleaner in place on each flower.

8. Wrap the opposite ends of the pipe cleaners together and glue to the back of the flowerpot. Allow the glue to set (follow the manufacturer's instructions).

9. Arrange your flowers by bending the pipe cleaners. Apply strong glue to the inside bottom edge of the card aperture. Position the pot behind the aperture and stick in place. With a glue stick, apply glue to the whole of the back of the aperture and stick the inner card to this, trapping the bottom edge of the pot inside.

Three-dimensional Christmas Tree

This very effective card, which is featured on pages 52–3,
looks much more complicated than it really is.
The festive air is completed with the addition of some
gold-coloured tinsel and a little cat bell.

1. Paint one piece of acetate Turquoise Blue and the other Light Green. Sprinkle Lazer silver glitter on to the wet paint and then use tweezers to place silver star sequins and clear hearts at random over the surface. Leave to dry for about 24 hours.

2. When the paint has dried, hold the traced template against the painted side of the acetate and cut out a tree shape. Repeat with the other painted acetate.

3. Cut a vertical line from the top of one tree shape to the centre of the tree, then cut a vertical line up the other tree shape from the base to the centre.

4. Slot the two tree shapes together to produce a three-dimensional tree.

5. Sew a bell to the top of the tree with invisible thread and fix the end of the thread to the inside top edge of the aperture with a sticker. Wrap tinsel around the thread and use glue to fix the tree sequins and 'Merry Christmas' to the front of the card.

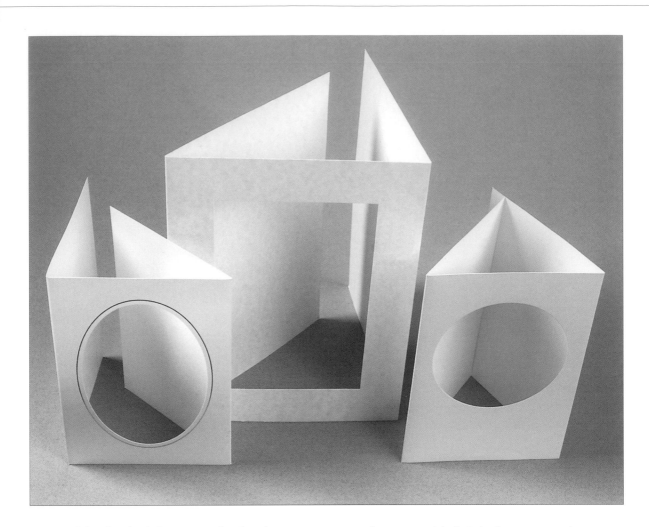

Most of the finished designs in this book are displayed in 'double-fold' cards. These consist of three panels of card joined together to form both a cover and a backing sheet for your greetings card. They are available in craft shops and department stores, and are complete with envelopes provided. It is, however, quite easy to make your own double-fold cards. This will give you the opportunity to choose different colours and surfaces. The actual dimensions for the card can be based on those which are given in each project.

To My Valentine

Valentine cards are a pleasure to send and to receive, and there can be no better way of showing someone you care than to make a card yourself. Whether it is used as a mobile or as a flat design the heart is ideal for cards such as these.

♥

Celtic Heart 24

Red Rose 25

Double Sequin and Confetti Heart 26

Double Red Heart 27

Square Heart 29

Pendent Hearts 30

Celtic Heart

DIMENSIONS

Design: Length 10cm (4in),
　width 8cm (3¹⁄₄in)
Whole card: Length 20cm (8in),
　width 15cm (6in)
Aperture: Length 14cm (5³⁄₄in),
　width 9cm (3³⁄₄in)

MATERIALS

* ❊ Acetate: OHP photocopy
　transparency sheet, template
* ❊ Bronze outliner
* ❊ 1 white double-fold greeting card with
　rectangular aperture, envelope
* ❊ Small round sticker
* ❊ Needle and invisible thread
* ❊ Small assorted coloured beads
* ❊ White spirit
* ❊ Paints: Pebeo Vitrail spirit-based – Orange 16,
　Crimson 12, Violet 25, Purple 26
* ❊ Paintbrush, scissors, tape

METHOD

1 Place the sheet of acetate over the template and
secure it to a flat surface with tape. Following
the outline of the design, apply the outliner to the
acetate. Leave to dry for about 2 hours.

2 When the outliner is dry, paint each section in the assortment of colours. It is important to paint up to the outliner, leaving no gaps. Leave to dry for about 24 hours.

3 Carefully cut around the outer edge of the design. Using the needle and a length of invisible thread, thread on four coloured beads of your choice. Stitch to the bottom of the heart and secure with a knot. Repeat this at the top of the heart, leaving extra thread to secure it to the card. At the top edge of the card aperture, position the thread at the centre of the inside edge and secure with a small sticker.

Red Rose

DIMENSIONS

Whole card: Length 15cm (6in),
    width 10cm (4in)
Aperture: Diameter 8cm (3¼in)

MATERIALS

* ✳ Acetate: OHP photocopy transparency sheet, template
* ✳ 1 white double-fold greeting card with round aperture, envelope
* ✳ Gold outliner
* ✳ Glue stick
* ✳ White spirit
* ✳ Paints: Pebeo Vitrail spirit-based – Crimson 12, Green Gold 22
* ✳ Paintbrush, scissors, tape

METHOD

1 Cut the sheet of acetate so that it is 3cm (1¼in) larger than the card aperture. Place the acetate over the template and secure to a flat surface with tape. Following the outline of the design, apply the outliner to the acetate. Leave to dry for about 2 hours.

2 When the outliner is completely dry, paint the design as shown and leave to dry for about 24 hours.

3 Apply glue to the inside edge of the aperture and, with the right side of the design facing outwards, position the acetate centrally over the aperture and stick in position.

Double Sequin and Confetti Heart

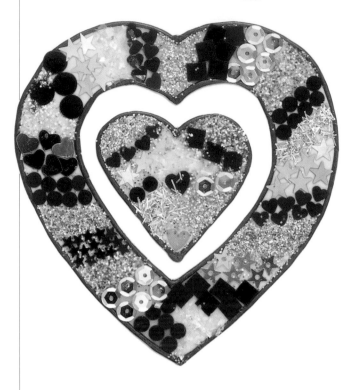

DIMENSIONS

Design: Length 9cm (3³/₄in),
 width 9cm (3³/₄in)
Whole card: Length 20cm (8in),
 width 15cm (6in)
Aperture: Length 10cm (4in),
 width 10cm (4in)

MATERIALS

* ✳ Acetate: OHP photocopy transparency sheet, template
* ✳ 1 white double-fold greeting card with square aperture, envelope
* ✳ Grey outliner
* ✳ Pebeo Vitrail clear varnish
* ✳ Assorted sequins in pink, silver and purple
* ✳ Lazer silver glitter
* ✳ Small white sticker
* ✳ White spirit
* ✳ Needle and invisible thread
* ✳ Paintbrush, scissors, tweezers, tape

METHOD

1 Place the sheet of acetate over the heart templates and secure to a flat surface with tape. Following the outline of the design, apply the outliner to the acetate. Leave to dry for about 2 hours.

2 When the outliner is dry, paint the two hearts with clear varnish and while still wet use tweezers to place clusters of the three shades of sequins around the large heart and evenly within the small heart. Leave to dry for about 24 hours.

Tip
When cutting out and handling painted
or varnished acetate hold a piece of paper
over the painted surface. This will
prevent fingerprints from
marking the surface.

3 When they are completely dry, cut around the two heart shapes. Using needle and invisible thread, attach the top edge of the small heart to the inside top edge of the large heart, pulling up the thread until the small heart is in the centre. Secure the thread with a knot. Then attach a length of thread to the centre top edge of the large heart and secure with a knot.

4 At the top edge of the card aperture position the thread on the inside top edge of the aperture and secure with a small sticker.

Double Red Heart

DIMENSIONS

Design: Length 9cm (3³⁄₄in),
    width 8.5cm (3¹⁄₂in)
Whole card: Length 14.5cm (5¹⁄₂in),
    width 14.5cm (5¹⁄₂in)
Aperture: Length 9.5cm (3³⁄₄in),
    width 9.5cm (3³⁄₄in)

MATERIALS

* Acetate: OHP photocopy transparency sheet, template
* 1 white double-fold greeting card with square aperture, envelope
* Grey outliner
* White spirit
* Small round sticker
* Needle and invisible thread
* 1 silver-coloured cat bell
* Paints: Pebeo Vitrail spirit-based – Crimson 12, Orange 16, Rose Pink 21, Yellow 14
* Paintbrush, scissors, tape

METHOD

1 Place the sheet of acetate over the template and secure to a flat surface with tape. Following the outline of the design, apply the outliner to the acetate. Leave to dry for about 2 hours.

2 To paint the design, begin at the centre, painting the small heart shape Rose Pink. Be generous with the paint to obtain a rich colour. Apply evenly placed dots of outliner to the narrow border between the two heart shapes.

3 Apply paint to the outer heart shape, beginning at the top and working in a clockwise direction. When the painting is finished leave it to dry for about 24 hours.

4 When it is completely dry, carefully cut around the heart shape. Using the needle and thread, attach the bell to the lower point of the heart. Secure with a knot. Attach a length of thread to the centre top edge of the heart. Place this thread inside the top edge of the aperture of the card and secure with a sticker.

Small Double Heart

A smaller version of the Double Heart design featured above can also be made. The method of painting and finishing the smaller design is exactly as the above design, but it does use a different colour sequence. Photocopy the above template and reduce to the size required.

DIMENSIONS
Design: Length 6cm (2¼in),
    width 5cm (2in)
Whole card: Length 11.5cm (4½in),
    width 9cm (3¾in)
Aperture: Length 6.5cm (2½in),
    width 6.5cm (2½in)

ADDITIONAL MATERIALS
∗ Paints: Pebeo Vitrail spirit-based – Deep Blue 10, Emerald Green 13, Orange 16, Egg Yellow 14, Crimson 12.

Square Heart

DIMENSIONS

Design: Length 6cm (2¹⁄₂in),
  width 6cm (2¹⁄₂in)
Whole card: Length 11cm (4¹⁄₂in)
  width 9cm (3³⁄₄in)

MATERIALS

* ✳ Acetate: OHP photocopy transparency
  sheet, template
* ✳ 1 pale pink double-fold greeting card
  without an aperture, envelope
* ✳ Silver outliner
* ✳ Heart sequins
* ✳ Lazer white crystal glitter
* ✳ Glue stick
* ✳ Paints: Plaid Gallery Glass water-based –
  Rose Quartz 15120, Peach Blossom 15106,
  Snow White 15123, Raspberry 15119
* ✳ Paintbrush, scissors, tweezers, tape

METHOD

1 Place the sheet of acetate over the template
 and secure to a flat surface with tape.
Following the outline of the design, apply the
outliner to the acetate. Leave to dry for about
2 hours.

2 When the outliner is dry, apply the Raspberry
 paint to the centre heart, making sure there
are no gaps for the light to shine through. Using
all the colours, paint the small squares in alternate
colours until the border is complete. While still
wet, sprinkle the central heart and border with the
glitter and use tweezers to apply the sequins to
alternate squares as shown. Leave to dry for about
24 hours.

3 When it is completely dry, cut around the
 square design. Position the acetate design
centrally on the front of the greetings card and
mark the corners. Apply glue to this area
of the card and stick the acetate in position.

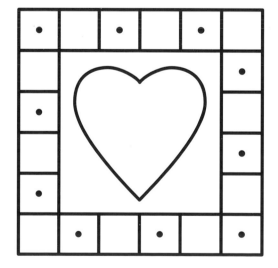

Pendent Hearts

DIMENSIONS

Design: Length 4cm (1½in),
  width 4cm (1½in)
Whole card: Length 11cm (4½in),
  width 9cm (3¾in)
Aperture: Length 6cm (2½in),
  width 6cm (2½in)

MATERIALS

* ❋ Acetate: OHP photocopying transparency
    sheet, template
* ❋ 1 white double-fold greeting card with
    square aperture, envelope
* ❋ Grey outliner
* ❋ Tiny red, yellow, blue and green beads
* ❋ Small round stickers
* ❋ White spirit
* ❋ Needle and invisible thread
* ❋ Paints: Pebeo Vitrail spirit-based – Rose
    Pink 21, Yellow 14, Deep Blue 10,
    Emerald 13
* ❋ Paintbrush, scissors, tape

METHOD

1 Place the sheet of acetate over the template and secure to a flat surface with tape. Following the outline of the shapes, apply the outliner to the acetate. Leave to dry for about 2 hours.

2 When the outliner is dry, paint the two heart shapes with the colours as shown. Leave to dry for about 24 hours.

3 When they are completely dry, carefully cut around the heart shapes. Using the needle and invisible thread, attach a length of thread to the top edge of each heart. Thread on the coloured beads, making one length of beads longer than the other. Make a knot in the thread so that the beads do not fall off. Position the ends of the threads on the inside top edge of the aperture and secure with stickers.

Option

Blank greetings cards are often available
with silver or gold borders.
The Pendent Hearts design shows a card
with a gold border.

Birthday Wishes

Birthday cards are sent to celebrate a special day.
Here is a collection of cards complete with
numerals templates.

14th Birthday 32

Birthday Initials 33

Birthday Teddy 34

Numerals Templates 38–9

18th Birthday 40

21st Birthday 41

30th Birthday 12

40th Birthday 43

14th Birthday

DIMENSIONS

Design: Length 6cm (2½in),
    width 7cm (2¾in)

Whole card: Length 15cm (6in),
    width 10cm (4in)

Aperture: Length 8cm (3¼in),
    width 8cm (3¼in)

MATERIALS

❋ Acetate: OHP photocopy transparency
    sheet, templates

❋ 1 white double-fold greeting card with
    square aperture, envelope

❋ Grey outliner

❋ Assorted silver-coloured star sequins

❋ 2 silver-coloured cat bells

❋ 2 small round stickers

❋ Needle and invisible thread

❋ Paints: Pebeo Porcelain 150 water-based –
    Lapis Blue 16, Ming Blue 17, Sapphire 18

❋ Paintbrush, scissors, tweezers, tape

METHOD

1 Place the sheet of acetate over the templates for numbers 1 and 4 and secure to a flat surface with tape. Following the outline of the numbers, apply the outliner to the acetate. Leave to dry for about 2 hours.

2 When the outliner is dry, paint the Lapis Blue, Ming Blue and Sapphire sections as shown. While still wet use tweezers to place the assorted star sequins in position.. Leave to dry for about 48 hours.

3 When completely dry, use the outliner to place swirls of outliner in the sections shown, and dots in the corners of the areas containing a single star. Leave to dry for about 2 hours. When the outliner is dry, carefully cut around the numbers.

4 Using the needle and invisible thread, attach a cat bell to the centre bottom edge of each number and secure with a knot. Attach a short length of thread to the centre top edge of each number and secure with a knot. Position the ends of these threads on the inside top edge of the card aperture allowing the numbers to hang centrally in the aperture. Secure each thread with a sticker.

Birthday Initials

DIMENSIONS

Design: Length 7cm (2³⁄₄in),
width 7cm (2³⁄₄in)
Whole card: Length 20cm (8in),
width 15cm (6in)
Aperture: Length 10cm (4in),
width 10cm (4in)

MATERIALS

* Acetate: OHP photocopy transparency sheet, template
* 1 white double-fold greeting card with round aperture, envelope
* Copper outliner
* Lazer crystal white glitter
* 1 gold-coloured cat bell
* 'Birthday' sequins in red and gold
* Red, shredded paper ribbon
* Small round sticker
* White spirit
* Needle and invisible thread
* Paint: Pebeo Vitrail spirit-based – Rose Pink 21
* Paintbrush, scissors, tweezers, tape

METHOD

1 Place the acetate over the template and secure to a flat surface with tape. Following the outline of the design, apply the copper outliner to the acetate. Leave to dry for about 2 hours.

2 When the outliner is dry, paint the design and then, while still wet, sprinkle with the crystal glitter. Using tweezers place the sequins in position. Leave to dry for about 24 hours.

3 When the paint is completely dry, carefully cut out the letter shape. Using a needle and invisible thread, attach the cat bell to the bottom of the letter and secure with a knot. Attach the thread to the top edge of the letter and secure with a knot. Position the thread on the inside edge of the aperture, allowing the letter to hang centrally in the aperture. Secure the thread with a sticker.

4 To decorate, shred the paper ribbon and curl over the blade of your scissors. Hang the ribbon by looping the curled ribbon around the letter and the supporting thread.

Birthday Teddy

DIMENSIONS

Design: Length 10cm (4in),
　　　　width 9cm (3¾in)
Whole card: Length 20cm (8in),
　　　　width 15cm (6in)
Aperture: Length 10cm (4in),
　　　　width 10cm (4in)

MATERIALS

* ✳ Acetate: OHP photocopy transparency sheet, template
* ✳ 1 white double-fold greeting card with square aperture, envelope
* ✳ Grey outliner
* ✳ Small sequins for cheeks (optional)
* ✳ 1 'Happy Birthday' sequin
* ✳ Glue stick
* ✳ White spirit
* ✳ Paints: Pebeo Vitrail spirit-based – Yellow 14, Orange 16, Crimson 12, Rose Pink 21
* ✳ Paintbrush, scissors, tweezers, tape

METHOD

1 Cut the acetate so that it is 15mm (⅝in) larger all round than the card aperture. Place the sheet of acetate centrally over the template and secure to a flat surface with tape. Following the outline of the design, apply the outliner to the acetate. Leave to dry for about 2 hours.

2 When the outliner is dry, paint the design with the colours shown, making sure that there are no gaps between the paint and the outliner. While the outliner and paint are still wet, use tweezers to place the 'Happy Birthday' sequin on the initial letter and, if you are using sequins, place these on the cheeks. Leave to dry for about 24 hours.

3 When the work is completely dry, apply glue to the inside edges of the card aperture and, with the right side of the design facing outwards, position the acetate centrally over the aperture and press down to secure. Stick down.

4 Cut lengths of the coloured paper ribbon and shred. Curl the ribbon with scissors. Place the ends of the curled ribbon on the inside top and bottom edges of the card aperture and secure each end with a small sticker.

Here is a selection of cards to suit a variety of birthdays. For those who do not care to divulge their age, send a card simply showing their initial!

Numerals Templates

To create your template either trace directly from these examples or,
if you need to alter the size of the final numerals by either enlarging or
reducing them, photocopy these examples
and alter the percentage of enlargement or reduction.

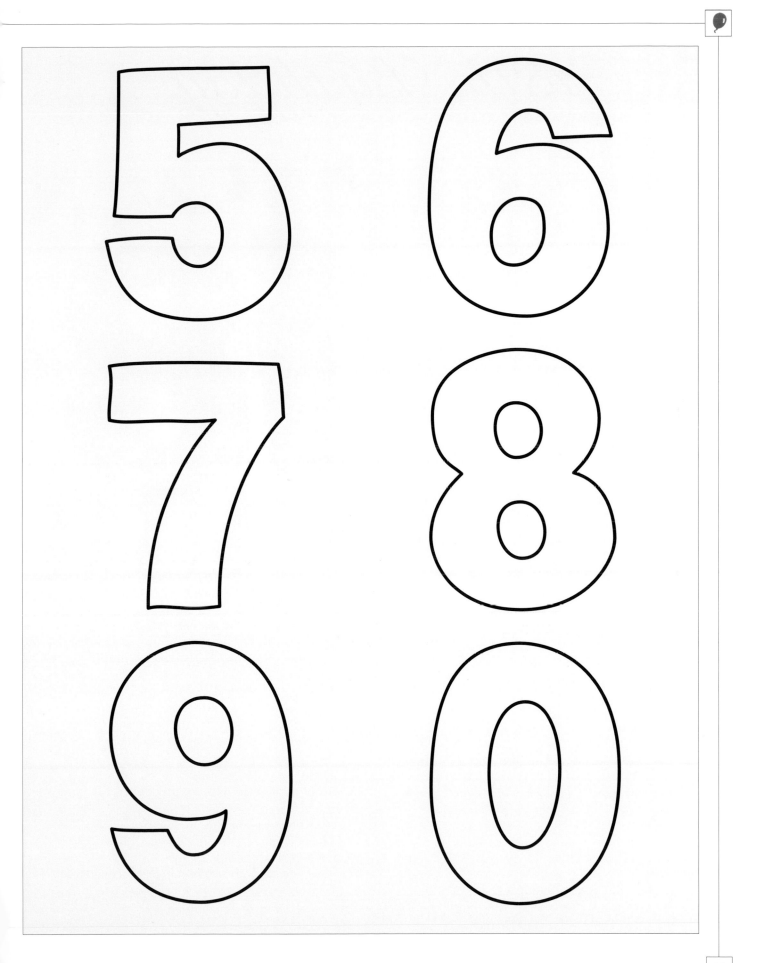

18th Birthday

DIMENSIONS

Design: Length 8cm (3¼in),
   width 9cm (3⅝in)
Whole card: Length 20cm (8in),
   width 15cm (6in)
Aperture: Length 10cm (4in),
   width 10cm (4in)

MATERIALS

* ❋ Acetate: OHP photocopy transparency sheet, templates
* ❋ 1 white double-fold greeting card with square aperture, envelope
* ❋ Grey outliner
* ❋ Lazer crystal glitter
* ❋ Assorted matt birthday party sequins
* ❋ 1 'Happy Birthday' sequin
* ❋ Flag sequins in assorted colours
* ❋ 2 small round stickers
* ❋ Needle and invisible thread
* ❋ Paint: Pebeo Porcelain 150 water-based – Emerald 19
* ❋ Paintbrush, scissors, tweezers, tape

METHOD

1 Cut the sheet of acetate so that it is 15mm (⅝in) larger all round than the card aperture. Position the templates of the numbers 1 and 8 side by side. Place the acetate over the templates and secure to a flat surface with tape. Following the outline of the numbers, apply the outliner to the acetate. Leave to dry for about 2 hours.

2 When the outliner is dry, paint the numbers in Emerald and while the paint is still wet, sprinkle the numbers with glitter. Use tweezers to place the 'Happy Birthday' sequin and assorted stars and dots on the paint. Leave to dry for about 48 hours.

3 Using the needle and a length of invisible thread, sew each flag on to the thread, attaching them at each corner and running the thread behind each flag. Position three or four flags pointing upwards and the remainder pointing downwards. When all are attached to the thread, drape the bunting from the inside top corners of the aperture, allowing it to hang slightly lower in the centre. Secure the ends of thread to the card with stickers.

4 When the numbers are completely dry, apply glue to the inside edges of the card aperture and, with the right side of the design facing outwards, position the acetate centrally over the aperture and stick in position.

21st Birthday

DIMENSIONS

Design: Length 8cm (3¼in),
width 9cm (3¾in)
Whole card: Length 20cm (8in),
width 15cm (6in)
Aperture: Length 10cm (4in),
width 10cm (4in)

MATERIALS

❊ Acetate: OHP photocopy
transparency sheet, templates
❊ 1 white double-fold greeting card
with square aperture, envelope
❊ Copper outliner
❊ Assorted silver, gold and orange
sequins
❊ 1 'Happy Birthday' sequin
❊ Lazer crystal glitter
❊ 2 gold-coloured cat bells
❊ Gold-coloured paper ribbon, shredded
❊ 2 small round stickers
❊ White spirit
❊ Needle and invisible thread
❊ Paint: Pebeo Vitrail spirit-based –
Orange 16
❊ Paintbrush, scissors, tweezers, tape

METHOD

1 Place the sheet of acetate over the templates of numbers 2 and 1 and secure to a flat surface with tape. Following the outline of the numbers, apply the outliner to the acetate. Leave to dry for about 2 hours.

2 When the outliner is dry, paint the numbers with the Orange paint, making sure that there are no gaps between the paint and outliner for the light to shine through. While the paint is still wet sprinkle with glitter and, using tweezers, place the sequins on the wet paint. Leave to dry for about 24 hours.

3 When they are completely dry, carefully cut around the numbers. Using the needle and invisible thread, attach a bell to the centre bottom edge of each number and secure with a knot. Cut two short lengths of invisible thread and attach these to the centre top edge of each number and secure with a knot. Position the threads on the inside top edge of the card aperture, allowing the numbers to hang centrally in the aperture. Secure each thread with a sticker.

4 To decorate, shred the gold paper ribbon and curl it by running it over the blade of your scissors. Wrap the ribbon around the threads suspending the numerals and allow them to hang down over the two numbers.

30th Birthday

DIMENSIONS

Design: Length 7cm (2³/₄in),
    width 10cm (4in)

Whole card: Length 20cm (8in),
    width 15cm (6in)

Aperture: Diameter 10cm (4in)

MATERIALS

* Acetate: OHP photocopy
    transparency sheet, templates
* 1 white double-fold greeting card
    with round aperture, envelope
* Grey and gold outliners
* 2 gold-coloured cat bells
* 20cm (8in) gauge 1 white cotton piping
    cord
* 2 small round stickers
* Needle and invisible thread
* White spirit
* Paints: Lefranc & Bourgeois spirit-based –
    Hiding White 004. Pebeo Vitrail spirit-
    based – Deep Blue 10, Crimson 12
* Paintbrush, scissors, tape

METHOD

1 Place the sheet of acetate over the templates
for numbers 3 and 0 and secure to a flat
surface with tape. Following the outline of the
numbers, apply the grey outliner to the acetate.
Leave to dry for about 2 hours.

2 When the outliner is dry, paint the Crimson,
Deep Blue and White sections as shown.
Leave to dry for about 24 hours.

3 When the paint is completely dry, apply
the grey outliner to the surface of the red
paint, marking a border of small dots close to
the inner lines and gold wavy lines across the
sections painted Deep Blue. Using grey outliner,
draw a small anchor shape on each white section. Leave to dry for about 2 hours.

4 When the paint is dry, carefully cut around
the numbers. Using the needle and invisible
thread, attach a bell to the centre bottom edge
of each number and secure with a knot. Cut two
short lengths of invisible thread and attach these
to the centre top edge of each number and
secure with a knot. Position the threads on the
inside top edge of the card aperture allowing the
numbers to hang centrally in the aperture.
Secure each thread with a sticker.

5 Tie a knot at each end of the white piping
cord. Tie the cord around the threads that
support the numbers with a loose knot. To
complement this design select a card with a
gold border.

40th Birthday

DIMENSIONS

Design: Length 6cm (2½in),
   width 5cm (2in)
Whole card: Length 14cm (5½in),
   width 14cm (5½in)
Aperture: Length 9cm (3¾in),
   width 9cm (3¾in)

MATERIALS

✳ Acetate: OHP photocopy transparency
   sheet, templates
✳ 1 white double-fold greeting card with
   square aperture, envelope
✳ Bronze, gold and copper outliners
✳ Assorted gold glitters
✳ Gold '40' sequins and assorted star
   sequins
✳ 2 gold-coloured cat bells
✳ Faber gold flakes No. 8781–99
✳ 4 small round stickers
✳ White spirit
✳ Needle and invisible thread
✳ Pebeo clear varnish
✳ Paints: Pebeo Vitrail spirit-based –
   Orange 16, Yellow 14. Pebeo Porcelain
   150 water-based – Gold 44, Copper 46
✳ Paintbrush, scissors, tweezers, tape

METHOD

1 Place the sheet of acetate over the templates
for numbers 0 and 4 templates and the
banner triangles template, and secure to a flat
surface with tape. Following the outline of the
numbers, apply the copper outliner to the
acetate. Following the outline of the seven banner
triangles, apply the gold, bronze and copper
outliners alternately to the triangles until the
seven are complete. Leave to dry for about
2 hours.

2 When the numbers are dry, paint the
sections between the lines of outliner with
the clear varnish. While it is wet, cover each
section with an assortment of gold glitter and
gold flakes. Using the tweezers, place the assorted
sequins randomly on the glitter. Leave to dry for
about 24 hours.

3 Paint the banner triangles alternately gold,
copper, orange and yellow until the triangles
are complete. While the paint is wet, use the
tweezers to place the '40' and the star sequins on
the paint. Leave to dry for about 24 hours.

4 When they are completely dry, cut around the numbers and the banner triangles. Using the needle and invisible thread, attach a bell to the centre bottom edge of each number and secure with a knot. Attach a short length of thread to the centre top edge of each number and secure with a knot and then attach the threads to the inside top edge of the card aperture, allowing the numbers to hang centrally in the aperture. Secure each thread with a sticker.

5 To complete the banner, using the needle and a length of invisible thread, thread each triangle in alternate colours on to the thread, attaching them at each corner and running the thread behind each triangle. When all are attached to the thread, drape the banner from the two top corners of the card across the numerals. Secure the ends of thread on the inside top edge of the card with stickers.

Happy Christmas

Capture the spirit of Christmas by creating these wonderful cards. The ideas range from sparkling mobile snowflakes and dazzling baubles, to a simple tree decorated with magnetic Christmas delights.

Christmas Tree 46

Christmas Bauble 48

Nine-square Patchwork 49

Five-strip Patchwork 50

Dove Bauble 51

Three-dimensional Christmas Tree 52

Snowflake 53

Christmas Tree

DIMENSIONS

Design: Length 13cm (5in),
   width 10cm (4in)
Whole card: Length 20cm (8in),
   width 15cm (6in)
Aperture: Length 14cm (5½in),
   width 9cm (3¾in)

MATERIALS

* ❋ Acetate: OHP photocopy transparency
  sheet, templates
* ❋ 1 white double-fold greeting card with
  oblong aperture, envelope or shallow
  box
* ❋ Black outliner
* ❋ Glue gun
* ❋ 5 small round lightweight magnets,
* ❋ Small wooden square beads of
  assorted colours
* ❋ White spirit
* ❋ Pebeo Vitrail clear varnish
* ❋ Paints: Pebeo Porcelain 150 water-based –
  Ming Blue 17, Parma 14, Fuchsia Pink 09,
  Saffron 03, Coral 05, Sapphire 18,
  Ruby 07, Emerald 19, Olivine Green 27,
  Ivory 43
* ❋ Paintbrush, scissors, tape

METHOD

1 Cut the sheet of acetate for the tree so that it
is 15mm (⅝in) larger on all edges than the
card aperture and use the remaining acetate for
the shapes. Place the two pieces of acetate over
the tree and shapes templates and secure to a
flat surface with tape. Following the outlines of
the tree and shapes, apply the outliner to the
acetate. Leave to dry for about 2 hours.

2 To obtain the colour for the tree, mix
together small amounts of the Emerald,
Olivine Green and Ivory until you have the
correct colour green. When the outliner is dry,
paint the tree with the mixed green paint.
Paint the base of the tree Ruby, the gift Coral,

the cracker Sapphire, the star Saffron, the heart
Fuchsia Pink and the stocking Parma. Leave to
dry for about 48 hours.

3 When the paint is dry, paint small spots of
Ming Blue randomly over the surface of the
tree and the background. Leave to dry. Apply a
coat of white paint to the wrong side of the
shapes. Leave to dry. Using the glue gun, stick
the coloured beads to the right side of the
shapes and a small magnet to the wrong side.

Paint the surface of the tree with clear varnish. Leave to dry for about 24 hours. Stick a small magnet to the right side of the blue spots on the tree and one at the base of the tree.

4 Carefully cut around the shapes only. Apply glue to the inside edge of the aperture and, with the right side of the tree design facing outwards, position the acetate centrally over the aperture and stick down.

5 Decorate the tree with the magnetic shapes and position them as you wish. This is a fun card for children to make and receive, but an adult should supervise the cutting out.

Christmas Bauble

DIMENSIONS

Design: Length 7cm (2¾in),
   width 7.5cm (3in)
Whole card: Length 15cm (6in),
   width 10cm (4in)
Aperture: Diameter 8cm (3¼in)

MATERIALS

❋ Acetate: OHP photocopy transparency
   sheet, template
❋ 1 white double-fold greeting card with
   round aperture, envelope
❋ Gold outliner
❋ 1 gold-coloured cat bell
❋ Short length of gold-coloured tinsel
❋ 1 small crystal jewel
❋ Star sequins
❋ Lazer crystal glitter
❋ Small round sticker
❋ White spirit
❋ Needle and invisible thread
❋ Pebeo clear varnish
❋ Paints: Pebeo Vitrail spirit-based –
   Emerald 13, Yellow 14, Crimson 12,
   Orange 16
❋ Paintbrush, scissors, tweezers, tape

METHOD

1 Place the sheet of acetate over the template
and secure to a flat surface with tape.
Beginning in the centre, follow the outline of the
design and apply the outliner to the acetate.
Leave to dry for about 2 hours.

2 When the outliner is dry, paint the small
centre circle with varnish and, while it is
wet, use the tweezers to place the jewel in the
centre. Paint the design, working from the
outwards. While the paint is wet, sprinkle with
glitter. Use the tweezers to place the sequins.
Leave to dry for about 24 hours.

3 When it is completely dry, carefully cut
around the bauble. Using the needle and a
length of invisible thread, attach the bell to the
top of the bauble and secure with a knot.
Position the remaining thread to the inside top
edge of the aperture, allowing the bauble to
hang centrally in the aperture. Hold in place
with a sticker.

4 To decorate, wrap the gold tinsel around
the thread so that it hangs down over the
bauble.

Tips

Use good quality sequins to decorate cards,
because cheap sequins may bleed into the wet
paint. When you apply outliner, keep the nozzle
slightly above the design and lay the outliner
on the acetate with a smooth action.

Nine-square Patchwork

METHOD

1 Cut the sheet of acetate 15mm (⅝ in) larger all round than the card aperture. Secure the acetate over the template with tape. Apply the outliner to the vertical lines first, and then complete by following the horizontal lines with the outliner. Leave to dry for about 2 hours.

2 When the outliner is dry, paint the three squares showing glitter with clear varnish. While it is wet, sprinkle each square with a different glitter. Shake off the excess.

3 Paint the remaining squares using the assortment of blue paints. While they are wet, use tweezers to place the Christmas sequins in the centre of the painted squares. Leave to dry for about 48 hours.

4 When completely dry, apply glue to the inside edges of the card aperture and, with the right side of the design facing outwards, position the acetate centrally over the aperture and stick in place.

DIMENSIONS

Design: Length 9cm (3¾in)
   width 9cm (3¾in)
Whole card: Length 15cm (6in),
   width 10cm (4in)
Aperture: Length 8cm (3¼in),
   width 8cm (3¼in)

MATERIALS

* Acetate: OHP photocopy transparency sheet, template
* 1 white double-fold greeting card with square aperture, envelope
* Grey outliner
* Lazer silver, crystal and gold glitter
* Christmas sequins
* Glue stick
* White spirit
* Pebeo clear varnish
* Paints: Pebeo Vitrail spirit-based – Turquoise Blue 17, Pebeo Porcelain 150; water-based – Ming Blue 17, Sapphire 18, Lapin Blue 16. Lefranc & Bourgeois spirit-based – Cyan 087, Blue 025
* Paintbrush, scissors, tweezers, tape

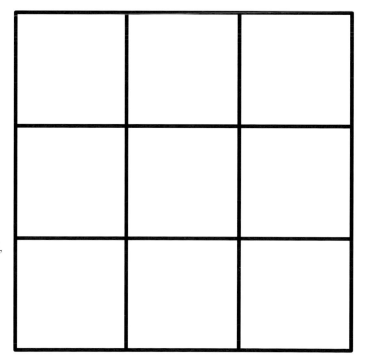

Five-strip Patchwork

DIMENSIONS

Design: Length 9cm (3³/₄in),
    width 9cm (3³/₄in)
Whole card: Length 15cm (6in),
    width 10cm (4in)
Aperture: Length 8cm (3¹/₄in),
    width 8cm (3¹/₄in)

MATERIALS

* ✳ Acetate: OHP photocopy transparency sheet, template
* ✳ 1 white double-fold greeting card with square aperture, envelope
* ✳ Gold outliner
* ✳ Assorted Christmas sequins and tiny silver stars
* ✳ White spirit
* ✳ Glue stick
* ✳ Paint: Lefranc & Bourgeois spirit-based – Purple 350. Pebeo Vitrail spirit-based – Emerald 13, Yellow 14, Crimson 12, Deep Blue 10
* ✳ Paintbrush, scissors, tweezers, tape

METHOD

1 Cut the sheet of acetate so that it is 15mm (⁵/₈in) larger all round than the card aperture. Place the acetate over the template and secure to a flat surface with tape. Following the outline of the design, apply the outliner to the acetate. Leave to dry for about 2 hours.

2 When the outliner is dry, apply the paint beginning at the top with Purple, then Crimson, Emerald, Yellow and Deep Blue down the left side of the design. While the paint is wet, use tweezers to place the Christmas sequins and silver stars as shown. Leave to dry for about 24 hours.

3 When it is completely dry, apply glue to the inside edges of the card aperture and, with the right side of the design facing outwards, position the acetate centrally over the aperture and stick in place.

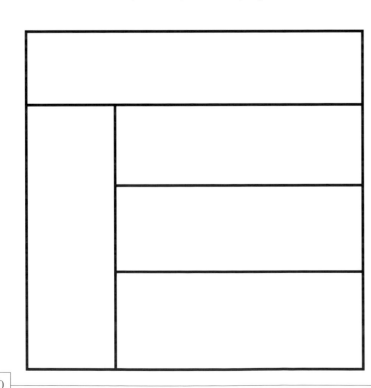

> ### Tip
> Always use tweezers to position sequins or beads on the surface of a design.
> When you are placing the Christmas sequins on this design, make sure that you place the single sequins centrally and the trees and holly in straight lines as shown.

Dove Bauble

DIMENSIONS

Design: Length 9cm (3¾in),
   width 8cm (3¼in)
Whole card: Length 14cm (5½in),
   width 14cm (5½in)
Aperture: Length 9cm (3¾in),
   width 9cm (3¾in)

MATERIALS

* Acetate: OHP photocopy transparency
   sheet, template
* 1 white double-fold greeting card with
   square aperture, envelope
* Grey outliner
* 2 silver-coloured cat bells
* Short length of narrow red ribbon
* Short length of thin gold tinsel
* Silver heart sequin
* Needle and invisible thread
* White spirit
* Paints: Pebeo Vitrail spirit-based –
   Deep Blue 10, Emerald 13. Lefranc &
   Bourgeois spirit-based – Hiding White 004
* Paintbrush, scissors, tweezers, tape

METHOD

1 Place the sheet of acetate over the template and secure to a flat surface with tape. Following the outline of the design and the lettering, apply the outliner to the acetate. Leave to dry for about 2 hours.

2 Beginning in the centre of the design, apply the paint to the acetate, making sure that the paint does not cover the outliner. While the paint is still wet, use tweezers to place a silver heart sequin in the centre of the dove. Leave to dry for about 24 hours.

3 When the paint is completely dry, carefully cut around the bauble. With the needle and a length of invisible thread attach the two bells to the top of the bauble and secure with a knot.

4 Tie the red ribbon around the bells and make a bow. Wrap the gold tinsel around the thread and let it hang down over the bauble. Using invisible thread, attach to the inside top edge of the aperture. Alternatively hang it from your Christmas tree, or in the window.

Three-dimensional Christmas Tree

* Glue stick
* White spirit
* Needle and invisible thread
* Paints: Pebeo Vitrail spirit-based –
    Turquoise Blue 17. Lefranc & Bourgeois
    spirit-based – Light Green 556
* Paintbrush, scissors, tweezers, tape

METHOD

1 Cut the sheet of acetate in half horizontally and put one piece to one side. Cut the remaining half in half vertically. Paint the two pieces of acetate, one in Turquoise Blue and one in Light Green. While the paint is wet, sprinkle with the glitter and use tweezers to place silver star sequins randomly on the paint. Leave to dry for about 24 hours.

DIMENSIONS

Design: Length 9cm (3³⁄₄in),
    width 9cm (3³⁄₄in)
Whole card: Length 14cm (5¹⁄₄in),
    width 14cm (5³⁄₄in)
Aperture: Length 9cm (3³⁄₄in),
    width 9cm (3³⁄₄in)

MATERIALS

* Acetate: OHP photocopy transparency
    sheet, template
* 1 white double-fold greeting card with
    square aperture, envelope or shallow box
* Lazer silver star sequins
* Lazer silver glitter
* 1 gold-coloured cat bell
* Short length of thin gold-coloured tinsel
* 1 gold 'Merry Christmas' sequin
* 4 green Christmas tree sequins
* Small round sticker

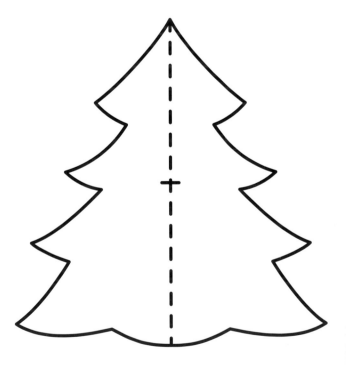

2 When the paint is dry, lay the template over the painted side of one piece of acetate and cut around the tree template shape. Repeat this for the second piece of painted acetate. Cut one tree shape from the top down to the centre and the second tree shape from the bottom up to the centre. Slot the two trees together along the openings to form a three-dimensional tree.

3 Using the needle and a length of invisible thread, attach the bell to the top of the tree and secure with a knot. Place the remaining thread to the inside top edge of the aperture, allowing the tree to hang centrally in the aperture. Secure in place with a sticker.

4 To decorate, wrap the tinsel around the thread and let it hang down over the tree. Using the glue stick, stick a Christmas tree sequin to each corner of the front of the card and the gold 'Merry Christmas' to the centre bottom edge.

Snowflake

DIMENSIONS

Design: Length 9cm (3¾in),
   width 7.5cm (3in)
Whole card: Length 14cm (5½in),
   width 14cm (5½in)
Aperture: Length 9cm (3¾in),
   width 9cm (3¾in)

MATERIALS

* ❋ Acetate: OHP photocopy transparency sheet, template
* ❋ 1 white double-fold greeting card with square aperture, envelope
* ❋ Grey outliner.
* ❋ Snowflake, silver stars and clear hearts sequins
* ❋ 1 star jewel
* ❋ Lazer silver glitter
* ❋ Small round sticker
* ❋ Glue stick
* ❋ White spirit
* ❋ Needle and invisible thread
* ❋ Pebeo Vitrail clear varnish
* ❋ Paintbrush, scissors, tweezers, tape

METHOD

1 Place the sheet of acetate over the template and secure to a flat surface with tape. Following the outline of the design, apply the outliner to the acetate, make sure that there are no gaps where the outliner joins. While it is wet, sprinkle with the glitter. Shake off the excess. Leave to dry for about 2 hours.

2 When it is dry, carefully paint the snowflake with clear varnish. While it is still wet, use tweezers to place the jewel in the centre of the design and the snowflake, silver star and clear heart sequins over the surface of the design as shown. Leave to dry for about 24 hours.

3 When it is completely dry, carefully cut around the design. With the needle and a length of invisible thread, attach the thread to the top of the snowflake and secure with a knot. Position the thread on the inside top edge of the aperture, allowing the snowflake to hang centrally in the aperture. Secure in place with a sticker. Using the glue stick, stick a snowflake sequin to each corner of the front of the card.
This design may also be used as a Christmas tree decoration.

Tip

If you find the outliner is flowing too quickly when you apply it to the acetate, place it in the refrigerator for a short while to harden slightly.

Happy New Year

Be prepared to celebrate the millennium
or any New Year.
Create these colourful and snazzy cards to send
your best wishes for the coming year to
your friends and family.

New Year 2000   56

Sun, Moon and Stars   58

New Year 2000

DIMENSIONS

Whole card: Length 20cm (8in),
   width 15cm (6in)
Aperture: Length 14cm (5¾in),
   width 9cm (3¾in)

MATERIALS

* Acetate: OHP photocopy transparency
   sheet, templates
* 1 white double-fold greeting card
   with oblong aperture, envelope or
   shallow box
* Silver outliner

* Lazer silver glitter
* Assorted moon and stars sequins
* Silver craft wire
* Small round stickers
* Glue stick
* Coloured paper ribbon, shredded
* Pebeo Vitrail gloss varnish
* Paints: Pebeo Porcelain 150 water-
   based – Ruby 07, Ming Blue Saffron
   03, Fuchsia Pink 09, Lapis Blue 16,
   Emerald 19, Coral 05, Parma 14
* Paintbrush, pencil, scissors, tweezers, tape

METHOD

1 For the rooftop shape, cut the acetate so that it is 7cm (2¾in) long by 18cm (7in) wide. For the numbers, cut the acetate to 13cm (5in) long by 5cm (2in) wide. Place the acetate for the rooftop shape over the template and also the acetate for the numbers over the number template. Secure both to a flat surface with tape. Following the outline of the letters for New Year and of the numbers 2000, apply the outliner to both pieces of acetate. While still wet, sprinkle with the glitter. Shake off excess glitter and leave to dry for about 2 hours.

2 When it is dry, paint the numbers. While the paint is still wet, use tweezers to place silver star and moon sequins on the numbers as shown. Leave to dry for 48 hours. Paint the letters in assorted colours and the complete background in Lapis Blue. While still wet, sprinkle with glitter and add the sequins. Allow 48 hours to dry.

3 Apply glue to the lower half of the inside edge of the aperture to match the size of the roof top acetate. With the right side of this design facing outwards, position the acetate centrally over the aperture and stick it in position.

4 Carefully cut around the numbers. Cut four pieces of silver craft wire, each approximately 34cm (13½in) long. Wind each length 10 times tightly around a pencil. These will form the springs that hold the numbers. Remove the wires from the pencil and bend three of the springs over at the top to hold each number in place. Secure the bottom end of the springs together by twisting the wires together. Spread the springs out into a fan shape.

5 Secure the springs to the inside bottom edge of the aperture, behind the roof top acetate, with stickers or tape. Slip each number into the top of the appropriate spring.

Tip
If you find it difficult bending the ends of the springs over to hold the numbers, stick the numbers to the tops of the springs using strong glue or varnish.

See page 60 for numerals templates

Sun, Moon and Stars

DIMENSIONS

Design background: Length 17cm (6½in),
width 12cm (4¾in)

Whole card: Length 20cm (8in),
width 15cm (6in)

Aperture: Length 14.5cm (5¾in),
width 9cm (3¾in)

MATERIALS

* ❋ Acetate: OHP photocopy transparency sheet, templates
* ❋ Silver hologram card
* ❋ 1 white double-fold greeting card with oblong aperture, envelope
* ❋ Silver and gold outliners
* ❋ Royal Talens bronze outliner
* ❋ Lazer white crystal glitter
* ❋ Star and 'New Year' sequin confetti
* ❋ Pebeo clear varnish
* ❋ Small round stickers
* ❋ Glue stick
* ❋ White spirit
* ❋ Coloured paper ribbon, shredded
* ❋ Needle and invisible thread
* ❋ Paints: Pebeo Vitrail spirit-based – Deep Blue 10, Egg Yellow 14, Rose Pink 21
* ❋ Paintbrush, scissors, tape

METHOD

1 Place the sheet of acetate over the sun, moon and star templates and secure to a flat surface with tape. Using the gold outliner for the star, silver outliner for the moon and bronze outliner for the sun, follow the outline of the designs and apply the outliner to the acetate. Make sure that there are no gaps where the outliner joins. Leave to dry for about 2 hours.

2 When the outliner is completely dry, paint the shapes. Leave to dry for approximately 24 hours. When it is dry, apply the swirls of silver outliner to the surface of the moon. Leave to dry for 2 hours. Carefully cut around the outer edge of the shapes.

3 Using a paintbrush and varnish, paint swirls of varnish and the tail of the shooting star directly on to the hologram card. Sprinkle with the glitter while it is still wet. Shake off the excess glitter. Use the varnish to stick the confetti to the card. Leave to dry for about 2 hours.

4 Using the needle and invisible thread, attach a length of thread to each shape and secure with a knot. Position the threads on the inside edge of the aperture and secure in place with stickers. Apply glue to the inside edge of the aperture and, with the right side of the hologram card facing outwards, position the card centrally over the aperture and stick down.

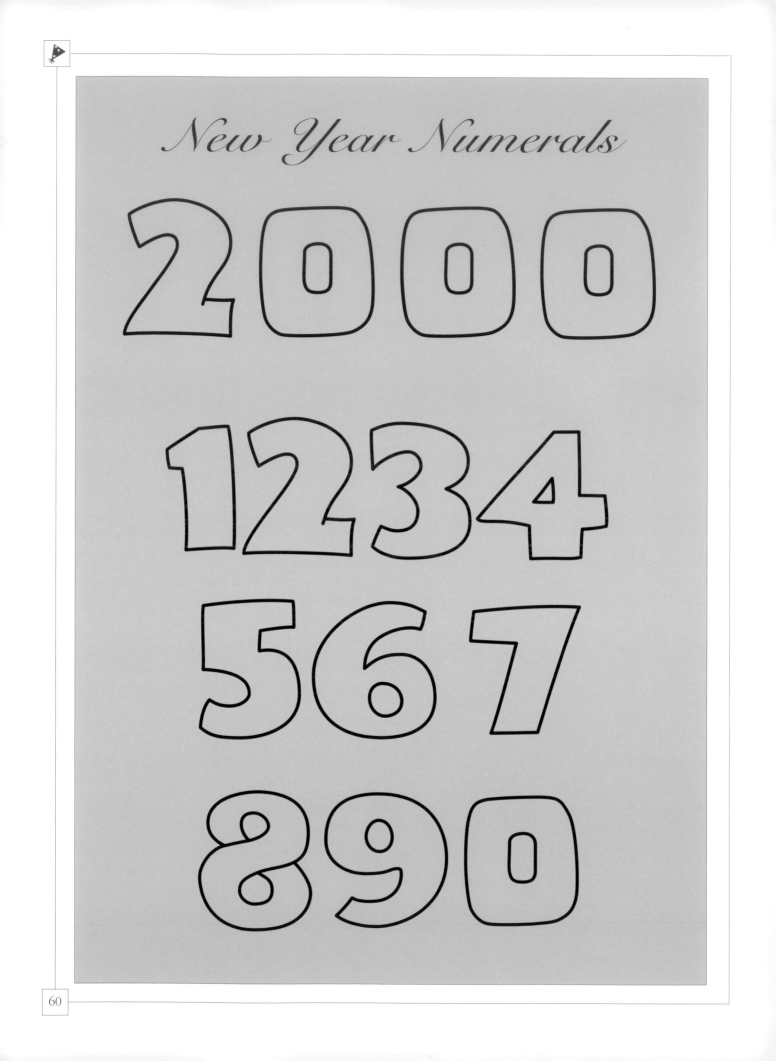

Easter

Send your message of Easter greetings with any
one of these delightful cards –
a daffodil to a parent, an Easter egg to a child,
or chicks and hearts to a loved one.

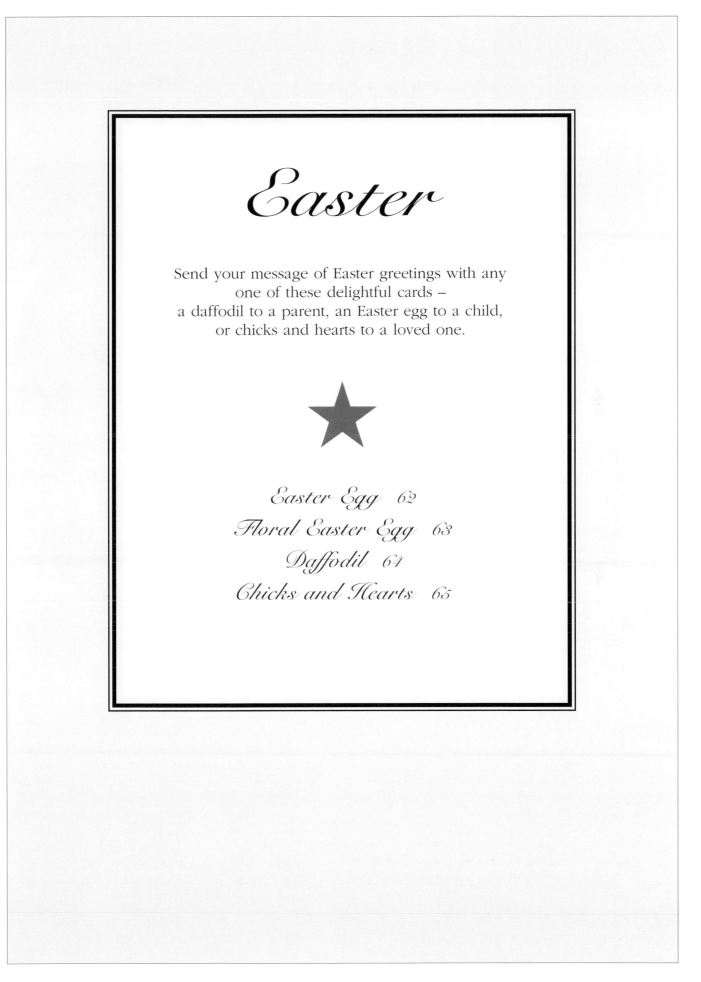

Easter Egg   62

Floral Easter Egg   63

Daffodil   64

Chicks and Hearts   65

Easter Egg

DIMENSIONS

Design: Length 12cm (4½in),
    width 8cm (3¼in)
Whole card: Length 15cm (6in),
    width 10cm (4in)
Aperture: Length 11cm (4½in),
    width 7cm (2¾in)

MATERIALS

* ❊ Acetate: for gift tag cut to size of template from a photocopy transparency sheet, templates
* ❊ 1 pale yellow double-fold greeting card with oval aperture, envelope
* ❊ Black outliner
* ❊ Gold outliner
* ❊ Glue stick
* ❊ Silver card
* ❊ Small piece of orange cellophane
* ❊ Small pieces of multi-coloured narrow ribbon
* ❊ White spirit
* ❊ Paints: Pebeo Vitrail spirit-based and Lefranc & Bourgeois spirit-based – your choice of colours
* ❊ Paintbrush, pinking shears, hole punch, tape

METHOD

1 Cut the silver card so that it is 15mm (⅝in) larger on all edges than the aperture of the greetings card. Place a tracing of the template over the silver card and secure to a flat surface with tape. Using a ball-point pen trace the design on the template, which will leave an impression on the silver card underneath. Remove the template. Following the impression of the design, apply the black outliner to the silver card. Leave to dry for about 2 hours.

2 Punch a hole in one end of the gift tag. With the gold outliner, write the words 'Easter Greetings' on the tag. Allow to dry for about 2 hours.

3 When the outliner on the card is dry, paint each section, using your choice of colours. Leave to dry for about 24 hours.

4 Apply glue to the inside of the card aperture and stick the painted card in place. Cut a piece of cellophane so that it is 10cm (4in) by 7cm (2¾in), cutting the longer edges with pinking shears to give a zigzag effect. Thread the coloured ribbon through the hole in the gift tag and tie once. Gather the cellophane up to form a bow. Tie the coloured ribbon around the centre to hold the gathers and secure the bow to the end of the gift tag. Attach the back of the bow to the top edge of the design with a small square of double-sided sticky tape.

Floral Easter Egg

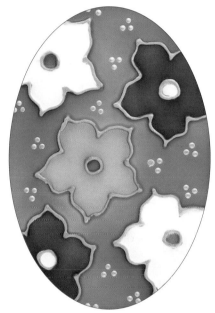

Easter Greetings

DIMENSIONS

Design: Length 10cm (4in),
width 7cm (2³⁄₄in)

Whole card: Length 11cm (4¹⁄₂in),
width 9cm (3³⁄₄in)

Aperture: Length 8cm (3¹⁄₄in),
width 5cm (2in)

MATERIALS

* Acetate: OHP photocopy transparency
  sheet, template
* 1 pale yellow double-fold greeting card
  with oval aperture, envelope
* Gold outliner
* Glue stick
* White spirit
* Paints: Pebeo Vitrail spirit-based –
  Orange 16, Lemon 23. Lefranc & Bourgeois
  spirit-based – Light Green 556, Hiding
  White 004
* Paintbrush, scissors, tape

Options
The cellophane used for the bow which
decorates the egg may be a different colour, and
the message on the gift tag, words of your own
choice.

METHOD

1 Cut the sheet of acetate so that it is 15mm (⅝in) larger all round than the card aperture. Place the acetate centrally over the template and secure to a flat surface with tape. Following the outline of the design, apply the gold outliner to the acetate. Leave to dry for about 2 hours.

2 When the outliner is dry, apply the paint, beginning with the flowers, in the colours shown. Then paint the background Light Green. Leave to dry for about 24 hours.

3 When the paint is completely dry, apply the outliner in small clusters of spots to the background as shown. Leave to dry for about 2 hours.

4 Apply glue to the inside edge of the card aperture and, with the right side of the design facing outwards, position the acetate centrally over the aperture and stick it in position.

Daffodil

DIMENSIONS
Design: Length 18cm (7in),
  width 13cm (5in)
Whole card: Length 20cm (8in),
  width 15cm (6in)
Aperture: Length 14cm (5½in),
  width 9cm (3¾in)

MATERIALS
 ✳ Acetate: OHP photocopy transparency
     sheet, template
 ✳ 1 large white double-fold greeting card
     with oblong aperture, envelope
 ✳ Copper outliner
 ✳ Glue stick
 ✳ White spirit
 ✳ Paints: Pebeo Porcelain 150 water-based
     Marseille Yellow 02, Saffron 03, Citrine
     Yellow 01, Coral 05, Olivine Green 27
 ✳ Paintbrush, scissors, tape

METHOD

1 Cut the sheet of acetate so that it is 15mm ($\frac{5}{8}$ in) larger on all edges than the size of the card aperture. Place the acetate over the template and secure to a flat surface with tape. Following the outline of the design, apply the outliner to the acetate. To obtain a rippled effect for the centre of the flower, place the nozzle directly onto the acetate and use a slight zigzag movement with the hand. Leave to dry for about 2 hours.

2 Apply the paint to the design. To create the tiny flowers scattered around the daffodil, use the tip of the paintbrush and paint to make tiny dots to form the shapes. Allow to dry for about 48 hours.

3 Apply glue to the inside edge of the card aperture and, with the right side of the design facing outwards, position the acetate centrally over the aperture and stick it in place.

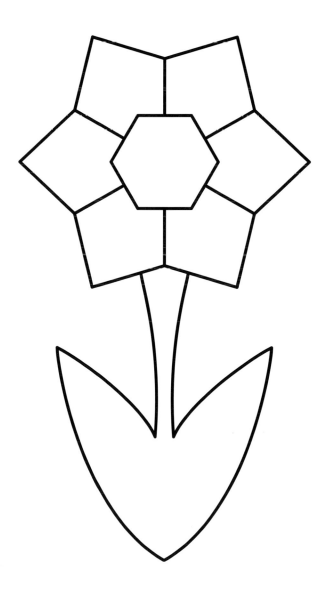

Chicks and Hearts

DIMENSIONS

Design: Length 10cm (4in),
width 3cm (1$\frac{1}{4}$in)
Whole card: Length 18cm (7in),
width 5cm (2in)
Aperture: Length 13cm (5in),
width 3cm (1$\frac{1}{4}$in)

MATERIALS

* Acetate: OHP photocopy transparency sheet, template
* 1 green double-fold greeting card with oblong aperture, envelope
* Small round sticker
* Needle and invisible thread
* 8 x 5mm gold-coloured rings
* 1 x 5mm gold-coloured cat bell
* Gold outliner
* White spirit
* Paints: Pebeo Vitrail spirit-based – Lemon 23, Yellow 14, Orange 16
* Paintbrush, craft pliers, scissors, tape

METHOD

1 Place the acetate over the templates and secure to a flat surface with tape. Following the outline of the chicks and hearts, apply the gold outliner to the surface of the acetate. Leave to dry for about 2 hours.

2 When the outliner is dry, paint the chicks and hearts in the colours shown, then allow them to dry for about 24 hours.

3 Using the needle and invisible thread, attach the small bell to the bottom edge of the largest heart. Secure with a knot. With the needle, make a small hole at the top of this heart and also at the top and bottom of the remaining hearts and chicks. Using the craft pliers, slightly open each gold ring and place one in each hole, except the top hole in the top heart. Close all the rings at the top edge of shapes and link the remaining rings at the bottom edges with these. Close the rings to secure.

4 Thread a small length of invisible thread through the hole of the top heart and fasten. Secure this thread to the top inside edge of card aperture with the small sticker.

Mother's Day

Tell your mother she is the best in the world
by sending her your special message
in a fluffy slipper or a funny flowers card.
Easy and fun to make for both children
and adults alike.

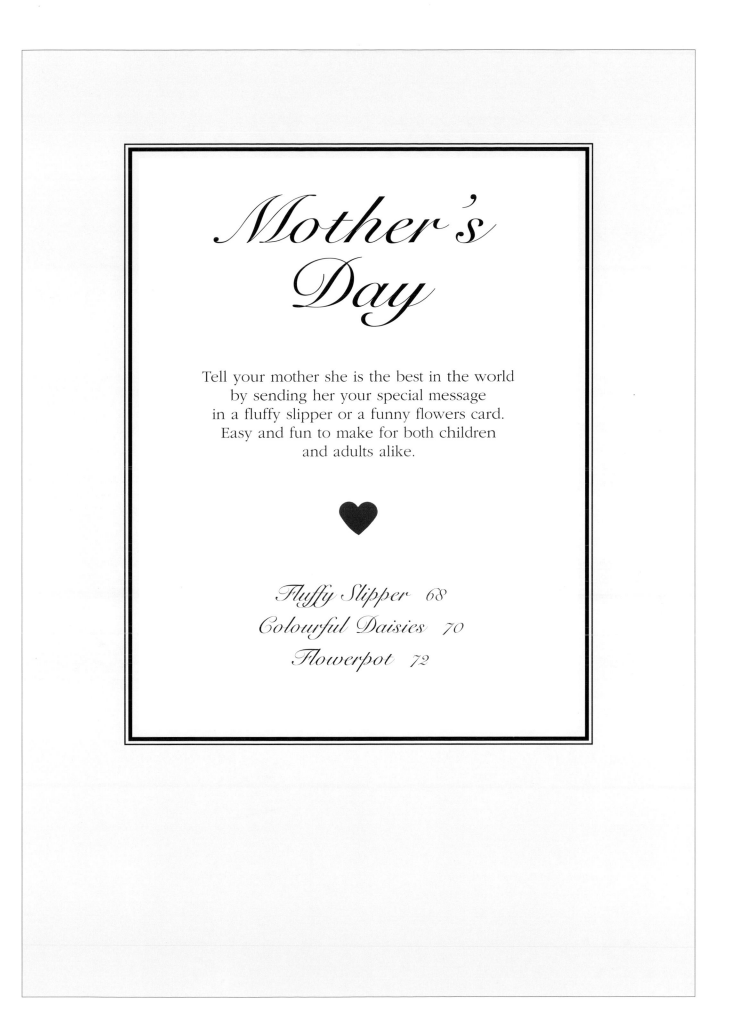

Fluffy Slipper 68
Colourful Daisies 70
Flowerpot 72

Fluffy Slipper

DIMENSIONS

Design: Length 9cm (3³⁄₄in),
   width 14cm (5¹⁄₂in)
Whole card: Length 10cm (4in),
   width 15cm (6in)
Aperture: Length 7cm (2³⁄₄in),
   width 11cm (4¹⁄₂in)

MATERIALS

* ❋ Acetate: OHP photocopying transparency
   sheet, template
* ❋ 1 cream double-fold greeting card
   with oblong aperture, envelope
* ❋ Gold outliner
* ❋ Lazer silver glitter
* ❋ Heart sequins and assorted beads
* ❋ 2 ostrich feathers, each measuring 5cm (2in)
* ❋ 2 small round stickers
* ❋ Glue gun or strong glue
* ❋ White spirit
* ❋ Needle and invisible thread
* ❋ Paints: Pebeo Porcelain 150 water-based –
   Gold 44, Purple 350. Pebeo Vitrail
   spirit-based – Orange 16
* ❋ Paintbrush, scissors, tweezers, hole punch,
   tape

METHOD

1 For the slipper shape, cut the sheet of acetate so that it is 15mm (⅝ in) larger all round than the card aperture. Place the acetate over the slipper template and secure to a flat surface with tape. Place the remaining acetate over the Mother's Day banner template and secure to a flat surface with tape. Following the outline of the slipper design and the Mother's Day lettering, apply the outliner to the acetate. Leave to dry for about 2 hours.

2 When the outliner is dry, paint the top edge of the slipper Orange and the wedge section Purple. While it is wet, use the tweezers to place the sequins on the wedge section. Leave to dry for about 24 hours.

3 To attach the ostrich feathers, twine them together and with the glue gun or strong glue stick them to the front of the slipper shape. Leave to dry.

4 When the glue is dry, cut around the banner shape and use the hole punch to make a hole at each end of the banner. With the needle and invisible thread, secure a length of thread through each hole with a knot. Thread five beads on each length of thread and secure with a knot.

5 Position the ends of thread on the inside top corners of the card aperture and secure with stickers, allowing the banner to hang across the aperture. Apply glue to the inside edges of the card aperture and, with the right side of the slipper design facing outwards, position the acetate centrally over the aperture and stick down.

> *Tip*
> Ostrich feathers can be bought
> by the metre or yard from most fabric shops,
> large department stores and
> good craft shops.

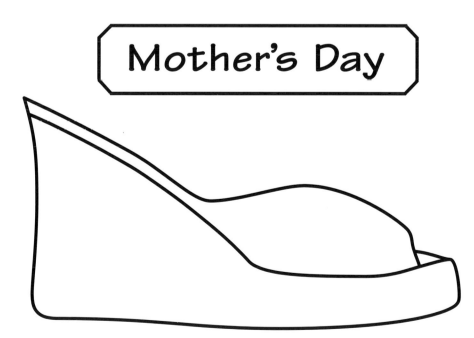

Colourful Daisies

DIMENSIONS

Whole card: Length 20cm (8in),
   width 15cm (6in)
Aperture: Length 10cm (4in),
   width 10cm (4in)

MATERIALS

* Acetate: OHP photocopy transparency sheet, template
* 1 white double-fold greeting card with square aperture, shallow box
* Silver outliner
* Lazer silver glitter
* 5 green pipe cleaners
* Glue gun or strong glue
* Glue stick
* Paints: Pebeo Porcelain 150 water-based – Lapis Blue 16, Coral 05, Ruby 07, Garnet 11, Saffron 03, Emerald 19, Parma 14, Azurite 15, Ming Blue 17, Fuchsia Pink 09
* Paintbrush, scissors, tape

METHOD

1 Place the sheet of acetate over the flower and pot templates and secure to a flat surface with tape. Follow the outline of the design and apply the outliner to the acetate to make five flowers and one pot. While it is wet, sprinkle with the glitter. Shake off the excess. Leave to dry for about 2 hours.

2 When the outliner is dry, paint the flowerpot Lapis Blue and the flowers Coral, Ruby, Fuchsia Pink, Garnet and Saffron. Paint the centres Emerald, Parma, Azurite, Ming Blue and Fuchsia Pink. Leave to dry for about 48 hours.

3 When the paint is completely dry, use a piece of paper to cover the surface and hold the acetate, and carefully cut around the flower and pot shapes. Cut each pipe cleaner to 12cm (4¾in) long.

4 Apply a spot of strong glue to the wrong side of each flower and stick one end of each pipe cleaner in place. Wrap the remaining ends of the pipe cleaners together and stick to the wrong side of the pot. Allow the glue to dry thoroughly.

5 Apply strong glue to the inside bottom edge of the aperture, and position the bottom edge of the pot centrally behind the aperture and stick in place. Using a glue stick, cover the whole surface of the wrong side of the aperture card, and stick the inner card to this, enclosing the bottom edge of the pot inside. Arrange the flowers as required by bending the pipe cleaners.

Tip

If you select your own range of colours for the flowers and the pot, make sure the paint is a dark tone or applied generously to the centres of the flowers and the bottom half of the pot. This will prevent the glue from showing through.

Flowerpot

DIMENSIONS

Design: Length 11cm (4½in),
   width 7cm (2¾in)
Whole card: Length 15cm (6in),
   width 10cm (4in)
Aperture: Length 11cm (4½in),
   width 7cm (2¾in)

MATERIALS

- ❋ Acetate: OHP photocopy transparency sheet, template
- ❋ 1 white double-fold greeting card with oblong aperture, envelope
- ❋ Grey outliner
- ❋ Glue stick
- ❋ White spirit
- ❋ Paints: Lefranc & Bourgeois spirit-based – Light Green 556, Cyan 087, Hiding White 004, Purple 350, Blue 025. Pebeo Vitrail spirit-based – Orange 16, Turquoise Blue 17, Yellow 14, Rose Pink 21
- ❋ Paintbrush, scissors, tape

METHOD

1 Cut the sheet of acetate so that it is 15mm (⅝in) larger all round than the card aperture. Place the acetate over the template and secure to a flat surface with tape. Following the outline of the design, apply the outliner to the acetate. Leave to dry for about 2 hours.

2 When the outliner is dry, paint the design, beginning with the flower, which is Rose Pink, and the centre, which is White; the leaves are Yellow and the pot Blue. The inner border is Light Green and the top and bottom borders are Turquoise and Orange. The side borders are Cyan and Purple. Leave to dry for about 24 hours.

3 When it is completely dry, apply glue to the inside edge of the card aperture and, with the right side of the design facing outwards, position the acetate centrally over the aperture and stick it in place.

Father's Day

Surprise your father on Father's Day
by creating a card especially for him.
The yacht and lighthouse designs
are colourful projects for both children
and adults to enjoy.

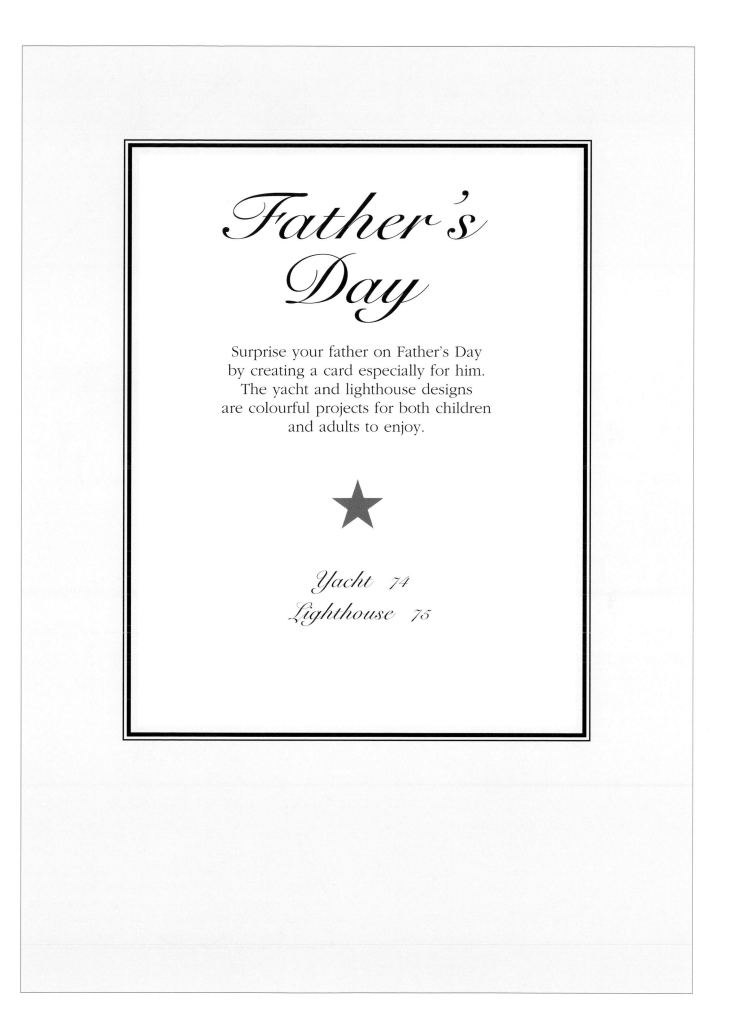

Yacht 74

Lighthouse 75

Yacht

DIMENSIONS

Design: Diameter 10cm (4in)
Whole card: Length 20cm (8in),
   width 15cm (6in)
Aperture: Diameter 10cm (4in)

MATERIALS

✻ Acetate: OHP photocopy transparency
   sheet, template
✻ 1 white double-fold greeting card with
   circular aperture, envelope
✻ Grey outliner
✻ Sequin stars
✻ Glue stick
✻ White spirit
✻ Paints: Lefranc & Bourgeois spirit based –
   Hiding White 004. Pebeo Vitrail spirit-
   based – Egg Yellow 14, Orange 16, Deep
   Blue 10, Crimson 12, Emerald 13
✻ Paintbrush, scissors, tweezers, tape

METHOD

1 Cut the sheet of acetate so that it is 15mm
   (⅝ in) larger all round than the card
aperture. Place the acetate over the template
and secure to a flat surface with tape. Following
the outline of the design, apply the outliner to
the acetate. Leave to dry for about 2 hours.

2 Beginning at the top of the card, paint the design using the colours as shown. Make sure that the paint is applied evenly and up to the outliner, leaving no gaps. While it is wet, use tweezers to place the sequin star on the sail. When finished, leave to dry for about 24 hours.

3 When it is completely dry, apply glue to the inside edge of the card aperture and, with the right side of the design facing outwards, position the acetate centrally over the aperture and stick in position.

Lighthouse

DIMENSIONS
Design: Length 12cm (4³/₄in), width 8cm (3¹/₄in)
Whole card: Length 15cm (6in), width 10cm (4in)
Aperture: Length 11cm (4¹/₂in), width 7cm (2³/₄in)

MATERIALS
* Acetate: OHP photocopy transparency sheet, template
* 1 white double-fold greeting card with oblong aperture, envelope
* Grey outliner
* Small silver star sequins
* Glue stick
* White spirit
* Paints: Lefranc & Bourgeois spirit based – Hiding White 004. Pebeo Vitrail spirit-based – Turquoise Blue 17, Deep Blue 10, Crimson 12, Black 15, Lemon 23
* Paintbrush, scissors, tweezers, tape

METHOD

1 Cut the sheet of acetate so that it is 15mm (⅝in) larger on all edges than the size of the card aperture. Place the acetate over the template and secure to a flat surface with tape. Beginning at the top of the design and following the outline, apply the outliner to the acetate. Leave to dry for about 2 hours.

2 When the outliner is dry, begin at the top of the design and apply paint to the acetate in the colours shown. Make sure that the paint is applied evenly and that there are no gaps for the light to shine through. While it is wet, use tweezers to place the star sequins on the background area. Leave to dry for about 24 hours.

3 When it is completely dry, apply glue to the inside edge of the aperture and, with the right side of the design facing outwards, position the acetate centrally over the aperture and stick in position.

Tip

If children are working on this project, have a roll of kitchen paper handy for cleaning brushes, wiping hands or mopping up any spillages that occur.

Avoid touching the surface of the painted acetate, because fingerprints will mark the design. When handling acetate, place a piece of paper over the surface of the design.

Bless the
Bride

A wedding is a happy occasion and a joy to watch.
From gorgeous gowns to colourful flowers,
from floating confetti to the peal of bells,
we love to celebrate this special day.
Your message of congratulations can be sent
with exquisite cards such as these.

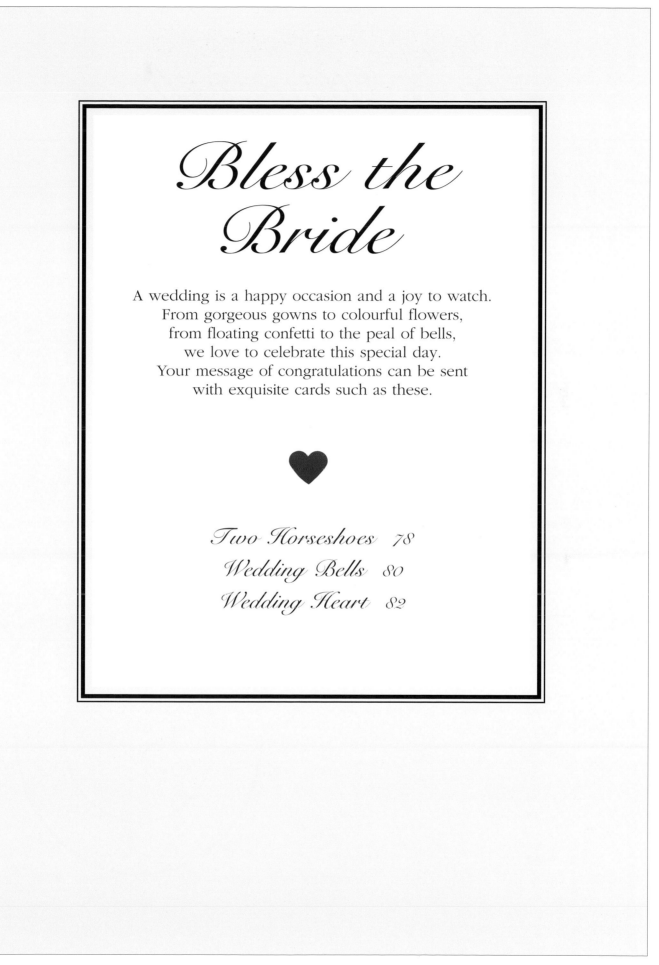

Two Horseshoes 78
Wedding Bells 80
Wedding Heart 82

Two Horseshoes

DIMENSIONS

Design: Measurements for each
horseshoe – Length 7cm (2³⁄₄in),
width 6cm (2½in)
Whole card: Length 20cm (8in),
width 15cm (6in)
Aperture: Length 10cm (4in),
width 10cm (4in)

MATERIALS

* ❉ Acetate: OHP photocopy transparency
sheet, template
* ❉ 1 white double-fold greeting card with
square aperture, envelope or shallow box
* ❉ Silver outliner
* ❉ Assorted wedding sequins
* ❉ 2 small white ribbon bows with pearls
* ❉ Narrow silver ribbon
* ❉ White paper ribbon, shredded
* ❉ Small pearl beads
* ❉ Glue stick or strong glue
* ❉ White spirit
* ❉ Paints: Lefranc & Bourgeois spirit-based –
Hiding White 004, Blue 025, Purple 350
* ❉ Paintbrush, scissors, tweezers, hole punch,
heart-shaped hole punch, tape

METHOD

1 To make the two horseshoes at the same
time, trace the template on to a second sheet
of paper. Cut the sheet of acetate horizontally in
half. Use the two halves for the two horseshoes.
Place the acetate centrally over the templates and
secure to a flat surface with tape. Following the
outlines of the horseshoes and small heart
shapes, apply the outliner to the acetate. Leave
to dry for about 2 hours.

2 When the outliner is dry, carefully cut
around the horseshoe shapes. Punch a small
hole in the ends of the horseshoes. Mix a small
amount of Blue, Purple and White paint together
to obtain a delicate shade of lilac. Paint the
entire background of the horseshoes, making
sure that the paint does not cover the outliner.
While it is wet, use tweezers to place the sequins
and small pearls in position. Leave to dry for
about 24 hours.

Tips

When you are mixing the paints to obtain the
delicate shade of lilac, mix a small amount of the
Blue and Purple together first. Then begin to
add the White, mixing in a little at a time,
until you have the correct shade of lilac.

Give yourself plenty of time to select and plan
the arrangement of sequins for decorating the
horseshoes.

The final touches are very important, and once
the sequins have been stuck down they cannot
be removed without damaging the design.

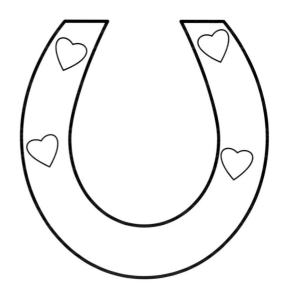

3 When completely dry, stick the small white ribbon bows to the bottom of the horseshoes. Cut two lengths of narrow silver ribbon and thread through the ends of the horseshoes. Punch two heart-shaped holes at the top edge of the card aperture. Twine one horseshoe around the other and thread one end of each ribbon through the heart-shaped holes. Pull up

to the required length and then secure the ends of the ribbons together to form loops, allowing the horseshoes to hang inside the aperture.

4 To decorate, shred the paper ribbon and curl it over the blade of your scissors. Place it around the ribbons and allow to hang down.

Wedding Bells

DIMENSIONS

Design, each bell: Length 6cm (2½in),
 width 6cm (2½in)
Whole card: Length 20cm (8in),
 width 15cm (6in)
Aperture: Length 10cm (4in),
 width 10cm (4in)
Pale pink background card: Length 13cm (5in),
 width 13cm (5in)

MATERIALS

* ✱ Acetate: OHP photocopy transparency
 sheet, template
* ✱ 1 white double-fold greeting card with
 square aperture, shallow box
* ✱ Pale pink card
* ✱ 2 silver-coloured cat bells
* ✱ Pastel-coloured pearl beads
* ✱ Silver heart sequins and clear star
 sequins
* ✱ Lazer crystal glitter
* ✱ White and silver paper ribbon,
 shredded
* ✱ Small round sticker
* ✱ White spirit
* ✱ Needle and invisible thread
* ✱ Glue stick
* ✱ Paint: Lefranc & Bourgeois spirit-
 based – Hiding White 004
* ✱ Paintbrush, scissors, tweezers, tape

METHOD

1 Place the sheet of acetate over the template
 and carefully cut around the shape four
times. Apply the paint to one side of each bell
shape. While it is wet, sprinkle with glitter and
use tweezers to place the sequins over the
surface. Leave to dry for about 24 hours.

2 When it is dry apply paint, glitter and
 sequins to the reverse side of the bell
shapes. Leave to dry again.

3 To avoid marking the decorated surface of
 the bell shapes with fingerprints, hold them
between a small piece of paper. Cut from the
top along the centre to the middle of two shapes
only. Then cut from the bottom along the centre
to the middle of the other two shapes. Slide two

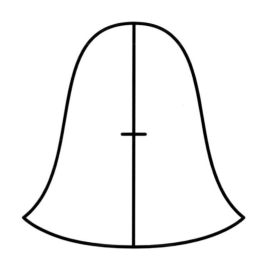

of the bells together along the openings, making
a three-dimensional bell. Repeat for the second
bell.

4 Using the needle and invisible thread, attach
 a cat bell to the bottom of each acetate bell,
and secure with a knot. Attach a length of thread
to the centre top edge of each bell and secure
with a knot. Thread small pearl beads on to the
threads, making one thread slightly longer than
the other.

5 Cut out the pale pink card to the size given.
 Apply glue to one side of the card and stick
this to the inside section of the greetings card,
so that it appears through the aperture when the
card is closed. Position the two threads on the
inside top edge of the aperture and secure in
place with stickers.

6 To decorate, shred the white and silver
 paper ribbon and curl it with scissors. Drape
the ribbon around the threads and let them hang
down over the bells.

Wedding Heart

DIMENSIONS

Design: Length 12cm (4³/₄in),
    width 10cm (4in)
Whole card: Length 15cm (6in),
    width 10cm (4in)
Aperture: Length 8cm (3¹/₄in),
    width 8cm (3¹/₄in)

MATERIALS

* ❋ Acetate: OHP photocopy transparency
    sheet, template
* ❋ 1 pale blue double-fold greeting card
    with heart-shaped aperture, envelope
* ❋ Silver outliner
* ❋ Lazer silver glitter
* ❋ Lazer crystal glitter
* ❋ Assorted wedding sequins
* ❋ Glue stick
* ❋ White spirit
* ❋ Pebeo Vitrail clear varnish
* ❋ Paints: Pebeo Vitrail spirit-based –
    Crimson 12, Deep Blue 10, Violet 25.
    Lefranc & Bourgeois spirit based –
    Hiding White 004
* ❋ Paintbrush, scissors, tweezers, tape

METHOD

1 Cut the sheet of acetate so that it is 15mm (⁵/₈in) larger on all edges than the card aperture. Place the acetate over the template and secure to a flat surface with tape. Following the lines of the design, apply the outliner to the acetate. Leave to dry for about 2 hours.

2 When the outliner is dry, apply varnish to the top right, middle and bottom left and right squares. While still wet, sprinkle the top and middle squares with crystal glitter and the bottom left and right squares with silver glitter. Shake off excess glitter. Using tweezers, place a 'Just Married' sequin on the middle square.

3 Mix pastel-coloured paints for the remaining squares by adding a little colour to the white paint. Paint each square and, while wet, sprinkle on a small amount of silver glitter. Shake off excess glitter. Use tweezers to place the sequins on the wet paint. Leave to dry for about 24 hours.

4 When the paint is completely dry, apply glue to the inside edge of the aperture and, with the right side of the design facing outwards, position the acetate centrally over the aperture and stick in place.

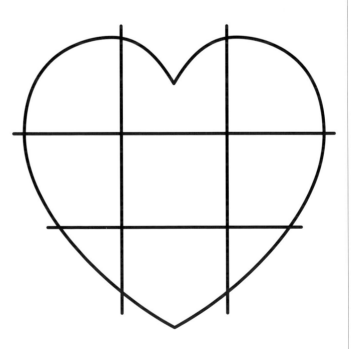

Happy Anniversary

Wedding anniversaries are celebrated in various ways, especially those that are recognized by a significant number of years together: Silver for 25 years, Ruby for 40 years, Golden for 50 and Diamond for 60 years. Here we celebrate the 25th anniversary with a numeral mobile which can easily be adapted for other anniversaries.

25th Wedding Anniversary   84

Anniversary Heart   86

Double Heart   87

25th Wedding Anniversary

DIMENSIONS

Design: Length 6cm (2½in),
    width 5cm (2in)
Whole card: Length 20cm (8in),
    width 15cm (6in)
Aperture: Length 10cm (4in),
    width 10cm (4in)

MATERIALS

* ❋ Acetate: OHP photocopy transparent
    sheet, template
* ❋ 1 white double-fold greeting card with
    square aperture, envelope or shallow box
* ❋ Silver outliner
* ❋ 2 silver-coloured cat bells
* ❋ Lazer silver glitter
* ❋ Assorted silver sequins
* ❋ 2 small stickers
* ❋ Needle and invisible thread
* ❋ White or silver paper ribbon, shredded
* ❋ White spirit
* ❋ Paint: Pebeo Porcelain 150 water-based –
    Peacock Blue 21
* ❋ Paintbrush, scissors, tweezers, tape

METHOD

1 Place the sheet of acetate over the template
and secure to a flat surface with tape.
Following the outline of the design, apply the
outliner to the acetate. While it is wet, sprinkle

the outliner with glitter. Shake off the excess
glitter. Leave to dry for about 2 hours.

2 When it is dry, paint the entire background
of the numbers with Turquoise Blue paint.
While wet, lightly sprinkle with glitter. Use
tweezers to place the assorted sequins on the
wet paint. Leave to dry for about 48 hours.

3 When it is completely dry, carefully cut
around the numbers. Using the needle and
invisible thread, attach a bell to the bottom edge
of each number and secure with a knot. Then
attach a short length of thread to the top edge
and position the threads on the inside top edge
of the aperture. Secure in place with small stickers.

4 Shred a length of paper ribbon and curl with
scissors. Place them around the threads and
allow to hang down.

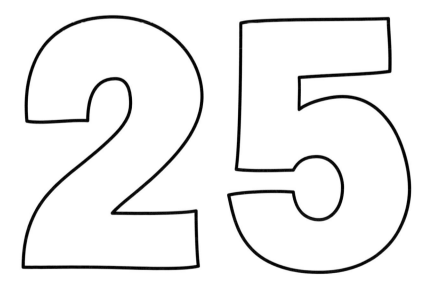

Anniversary Heart

DIMENSIONS

Design: Length 9cm (3¾in),
    width 8cm (3¼in)
Whole card: Length 20cm (8in),
    width 15cm (6in)
Aperture: Length 10cm (4in),
    width 10cm (4in)

MATERIALS

* Acetate: OHP photocopy transparency
    sheet, templates
* 1 white double-fold greeting card with
    square aperture, envelope
* Grey outliner
* Lazer silver glitter
* Assorted silver and anniversary
    sequins
* Plastic crystal jewels – hearts and stars
* Silver glitter and silver stars
* Needle and invisible thread
* White spirit
* Small round sticker
* Pebeo Vitrail clear varnish
* Paintbrush, scissors, tweezers, tape

METHOD

1 Place the sheet of acetate over the large heart and small heart templates and secure to a flat surface with tape. Following the outline of the designs, apply the outliner to the acetate. While wet, sprinkle with Lazer silver glitter. Shake off excess glitter. Leave to dry for about 2 hours.

2 When it is dry, paint the large heart with clear varnish and while wet apply the crystal hearts and stars as shown. Use tweezers to place the assorted silver sequins to cover the shape. Paint the small heart with varnish and, while wet, apply a 'Happy Anniversary' sequin in the centre as shown. Leave the hearts to dry for about 24 hours.

3 When both hearts are completely dry, carefully cut around each one. Using the needle and invisible thread, attach the top edge of the small heart to the inside top edge of the large heart, and let it hang in the centre of the large heart. Attach a length of thread to the centre top edge of the large heart and secure with a knot. Position the thread on the inside top edge of the aperture and secure in place with a small sticker.

Double Heart

DIMENSIONS

Design: Length 9cm (3³⁄₄in),
  width 9cm (3³⁄₄in)
Whole card: Length 20cm (8in),
  width 15cm (6in)
Aperture: Length 10cm (4in),
  width 10cm (4in)

MATERIALS

* Acetate: OHP photocopy transparency sheet, template
* 1 white double-fold greeting card with oblong aperture, envelope
* Gold outliner
* Small round sticker
* White spirit
* Needle and invisible thread
* 1 gold-coloured bell
* Paints: Plaid Gallery Glass water-based – Peach Blossom 15106, Rose Quartz 15120, Snow White 15123, Raspberry 15119
* Paintbrush, scissors, tape

METHOD

1 Place the sheet of acetate over the template and secure to a flat surface with tape. Following the outline of the design, apply the outliner to the acetate. Make sure that there are no gaps at the point where the outlining joins. Leave to dry for about 2 hours.

2 To paint the design, begin at the centre, painting the small heart shape Rose Quartz. Be generous with the paint to obtain a rich colour. Apply evenly spaced outliner dots to the narrow border between the two heart shapes.

3 Apply paint to the outer heart shape. Beginning at the top and working in a clockwise direction, paint each triangle with the four colours, repeating them as you work around the shape. While wet sprinkle with crystal glitter and apply heart and star sequins. Leave to dry for about 48 hours.

4 When it is completely dry, carefully cut around the heart shape. Using the needle and thread, attach the beads to the lower point of the heart. Secure with a knot. Attach a length of thread to the centre top edge of the heart and thread more beads and secure with a knot. Place this thread inside the top edge of the aperture and secure with a sticker.

New Baby

Celebrate the birth of
someone special by sending your
message of welcome
with one of these delightful cards.

Sweetheart Shoes 90

Stork 91

Sweetheart Shoes

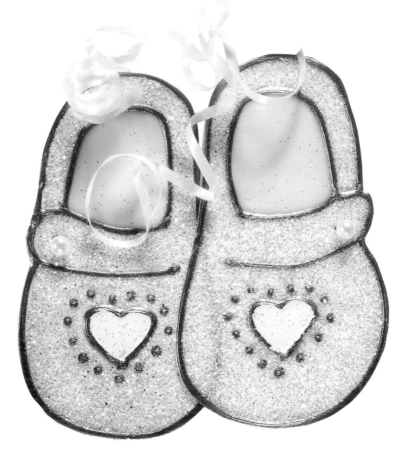

DIMENSIONS

Design: Length of each shoe
7cm (2¾ in), width of each
shoe 4cm (1½ in)

Whole card: Length 15cm (6in),
width 10 cm (4in)

Aperture: Length 8cm (3¼ in),
width 8cm (3¼ in)

MATERIALS

* Acetate: OHP photocopy transparency
   sheet, template
* 1 yellow double-fold greeting card
   with square aperture, envelope
* Bronze outliner
* Pearl beads
* Lazer white glitter
* Needle and invisible thread

* 2 small round stickers
* White paper ribbon, shredded
* Vitrail varnish
* White spirit
* Paint: Lefranc & Bourgeois Vitrail spirit-
   based – Hiding White 004. Gallery
   Glass water-based – Peach Blossom
   15106
* Paintbrush, scissors, tape

METHOD

1 Place the sheet of acetate over the template
and secure to a flat surface with tape.
Following the outline of the design, apply the
outliner to the acetate. Leave to dry for 2 hours.

2 When it is dry, leave the inside of the shoes
and the heart shapes unpainted and paint

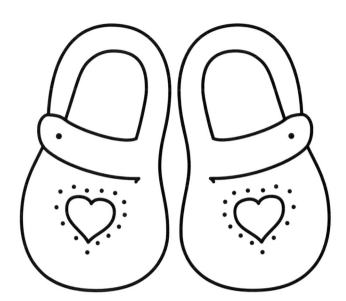

the remainder of the shoes with varnish. While still wet, sprinkle with Lazer white glitter. Paint the hearts white and the inside of the shoes Peach Blossom. Leave to dry for about 24 hours.

3 Carefully cut around the outer edge of the shoes. Using a needle and invisible thread, sew a pearl to each shoe for the fastener and secure with a knot. Also attach a short length of thread to the heel of each shoe. Secure the end of each thread to the inside top edge of the card with a sticker.

4 To decorate, shred a length of white paper ribbon and curl with the blade of your scissors. Place this around each thread at the heel of each shoe.

Stork

DIMENSIONS

Design: Length 13cm (5in),
    width 9cm (3³/₄in)
Whole card: Length 15cm (6in),
    width 10cm (4in)
Aperture: Length 11cm (4¹/₂in),
    width 7cm (2³/₄in)

MATERIALS

* ❊ Acetate: OHP photocopy transparency sheet, template
* ❊ 1 white double-fold greeting card with oblong aperture, envelope
* ❊ Silver outliner
* ❊ Baby confetti sequins
* ❊ Glue stick
* ❊ Lazer white glitter
* ❊ Vitrail clear varnish
* ❊ White spirit
* ❊ Paints: Lefranc & Bourgeois Vitrail spirit-based – Hiding White 004. Pebeo Vitrail spirit-based – Egg Yellow 14. Gallery Glass water-based – Rose Quartz 15120, Peach Blossom 15106
* ❊ Paintbrush, tweezers, scissors, tape

METHOD

1 Cut the sheet of acetate so that it is 15mm (⅝ in) larger on all edges than the size of the card aperture. Place the acetate over the template and secure to a flat surface with tape. Using the silver outliner, follow the outline of the design. Leave to dry for about 2 hours.

2 When the outliner is dry, paint around the outer area of the design with varnish. While it is wet, sprinkle this area with white Lazer glitter and place baby confetti sequins.

3 Paint the remainder of the design right up to the outliner and leave no gaps. Allow to dry for about 24 hours.

4 Apply glue to the inside edge of the aperture and, with the right side of the design facing outwards, position the acetate centrally over the aperture and stick down.

Option
The blanket shape held in the stork's beak may be painted in a colour of your choice.

Tip
Sequins are easily put in position with craft tweezers. Do this while the paint or varnish is still wet. If the paint has dried, use clear varnish over the painted area then position the sequins.

Home
Sweet Home

After moving house what could be
more welcoming than a specially made card?
Choose one of the designs shown here or
adapt one of the other patterns
in this book to greet friends
in their new home

Home Sweet Home 94
New Home 95

Home Sweet Home

DIMENSIONS

Design: Length 8cm (3¼in),
    width 8cm (3¼in),
Whole card: Length 15cm (6in),
    width 10cm (4in)
Aperture: Length 8cm (3¼in),
    width 8cm (3¼in)

MATERIALS

✳ Acetate: OHP photocopy
    transparency sheet, template
✳ 1 white double-fold greeting card
    with square aperture, envelope
✳ Silver outliner
✳ Small pink hearts, clear hearts,
    stars and letter sequins
✳ White spirit
✳ Glue stick
✳ Paints: Pebeo Vitrail spirit-based –
    Light Green 556. Pebeo Porcelain 150
    water-based – Coral 05, Ruby 07,
    Parma 14, Saffron 03
✳ Paintbrush, scissors, tweezers, tape

METHOD

1 Cut the sheet of acetate so that it is 15mm (⅝in) larger all round than the card aperture. Place the acetate over the template and secure to a flat surface with tape. Following the outline of the design, apply the outliner to the acetate. Leave to dry for about 2 hours.

2 When the outliner is dry, paint the squares as shown, using one colour at a time.

While the paint is wet, use tweezers to place the sequin shapes and letters in the centre of the squares as shown. Leave to dry for about 48 hours.

3 When it is completely dry, apply glue to the inside edges of the card aperture and, with the right side of the design facing outwards, position the acetate centrally over the aperture and stick in position.

> *Tip*
> When you are applying the outliner to the acetate complete all the vertical lines first. Then turn the acetate 90° and complete the horizontal lines.

New Home

DIMENSIONS

Design: Length 13cm (5in),
width 8.5cm (3½in)
Whole card: Length 20cm (8in),
width 15cm (6in)
Aperture: Length 10cm (4in),
width 7cm (2¾in)

MATERIALS

* Acetate: OHP photocopy transparency sheet, template
* 1 white double-fold greeting card with oblong aperture, envelope
* Silver and grey outliners
* Clear heart sequins
* Real sand and turquoise gouache paint (optional)
* White spirit
* Glue stick
* Paints: Lefranc & Bourgeois spirit-based – Light Green 556, Hiding White 004. Pebeo Vitrail spirit-based – Gold Green 22. Deep Blue 10, Orange 16, Crimson 12, Emerald 13
* Paintbrush, scissors, tape

METHOD

1 Cut the sheet of acetate so that it is 15mm (⅝ in) larger all round than the card aperture. Place the acetate over the template and secure to a flat surface with tape. Following the outline of the design, apply the grey outliner to the acetate. Leave to dry for 2 hours.

2 If you are using real sand on the lawn section of the design, mix the sand with a small amount of turquoise gouache paint and leave this to dry. When the outliner is dry, paint the design, beginning with the house. Paint the windows and door Hiding White, the house Crimson and the roof Orange. The surrounding hills and lawn are Light Green, Gold Green and Emerald, and the sky is Deep Blue. While the paint is wet, use tweezers to place two clear hearts coming out of each chimney. If you are using coloured sand sprinkle this on to the

front lawn section as shown. Leave to dry for about 24 hours.

3 When it is dry, follow the lettering on the template and apply the silver outliner to the painted surface. Write the words 'New Home'. Leave to dry for about 2 hours.

4 When it is completely dry, apply glue to the inside edges of the card aperture and, with the right side of the design facing outwards, position the acetate centrally over the aperture and stick in place.

Option
The use of the coloured sand as a different texture is optional. If you have difficulty obtaining sand, use coloured glitter.

Good Luck
&
Bon Voyage

The four-leaved clover is a recognized symbol for good luck. Send your good luck message to someone who is taking an exam, having an interview or travelling abroad. Used as a mobile or flat design, these simple but effective cards are ideal for any occasion.

Four-leaved Clover 98

Four-leaved Clover Mosaic 99

Palm Beach 101

Four-leaved Clover

DIMENSIONS

Design: Length 8cm (3¼in),
   width 8cm (3¼in).
Whole card: Length 15cm (6in),
   width 10cm (4in).
Aperture: Diameter 8cm (3¼in)

MATERIALS

 ❋ Acetate: OHP photocopy transparency
   sheet, template
 ❋ A white double-fold greeting card with
   round aperture, envelope
 ❋ Grey outliner
 ❋ Assorted green sequins and tiny green
   beads
 ❋ Lazer crystal glitter (optional)
 ❋ White spirit
 ❋ Small white sticker
 ❋ Needle and invisible thread

 ❋ Paints: Pebeo Vitrail spirit-based – Green
   Gold 22, Emerald 13, Turquoise Blue 17,
   Light Green 556
 ❋ Paintbrush, scissors, tweezers, tape

METHOD

1 Place the sheet of acetate over the template
 and secure to a flat surface with tape.
Following the outline of the design, apply the
outliner to the acetate, making sure that there
are no gaps where the outliner joins. Leave to
dry for about 2 hours.

2 Select the sequins and arrange them on a
 piece of paper to give a kaleidoscopic effect.
Beginning at the centre of the clover design,
paint the eight sections in alternate Light Green
and Turquoise Blue. While the paint is still wet,
use tweezers to place the sequins on these

sections in the arrangement chosen. Paint the remaining eight outer sections in alternate Green Gold and Emerald. While wet, place the remaining sequins on the paint. Leave to dry for about 24 hours.

3 When the paint is completely dry, carefully cut around the clover shape. Using the needle and invisible thread, attach a length thread to the centre outer edge of a clover leaf. Secure with a knot. Position the thread on the inside top edge of the aperture and secure in place with a small sticker.

Four-leaved Clover Mosaic

DIMENSIONS

Design: Length 12cm (4¾in),
   width 11cm (4½in)
Whole card: Length 14cm (5½in),
   width 14cm (5½in)
Aperture: Length 9cm (3¾in),
   width 9cm (3¾in)

MATERIALS

* ✳ Acetate: OHP photocopy transparency
     sheet, template
* ✳ 1 white double-fold greeting card with
     square aperture, envelope
* ✳ Gold outliner
* ✳ Faber gold flakes No. 8781–99
* ✳ Glue stick
* ✳ White spirit
* ✳ Pebeo clear varnish
* ✳ Paints: Pebeo Vitrail spirit-based –
     Deep Blue 10, Turquoise Blue 17,
     Emerald 13, Green Gold 22. Lefranc &
     Bourgeois spirit-based – Hiding White
     004, Light Green 556, Cyan 087
* ✳ Paintbrush, scissors, tweezers, tape

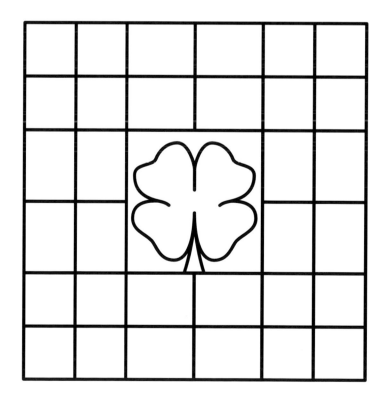

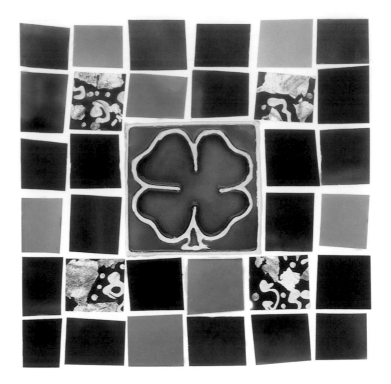

METHOD

1 Cut the sheet of acetate so that it is 15mm (⅝in) larger all round than the card aperture. Place the acetate centrally over the template and secure to a flat surface with tape. Following the outline of the central clover, apply the outliner to the acetate. Leave to dry for about 2 hours.

2 Cut five strips of acetate, each measuring 4cm (1½in) by 12cm (4¾in). Paint each strip using the colours Deep Blue, Turquoise Blue, Emerald, Light Green and Cyan. Leave to dry for about 24 hours.

3 When the outliner is dry, paint the clover Green Gold and the small surrounding square Turquoise Blue. Leave to dry for about 24 hours.

4 When the painted strips are dry, cut out several squares measuring 15mm (⅝in) square, with one or two slightly imperfect in size, from each colour. As a guide, the template may be used for this step, placing it over the painted surface and cutting out the squares. Paint any four of the small squares with clear varnish and, while it is wet, use tweezers to place small pieces of gold flakes and spots of outliner on to the surface. Allow to dry. Place the small squares of coloured acetate on a plain piece of paper, arranging them in a mosaic design and positioning the four decorated squares as shown

5 When the clover design is dry, apply Hiding White paint to the entire background of the large acetate square. While it is still wet, use tweezers to place the small painted squares on the surface of the paint, in the preselected arrangement. Leave small spaces between the squares so that the white background shows, thus providing a mosaic effect. Leave to dry for about 24 hours.

6 When the design is completely dry, apply glue to the inside edges of the card aperture and, with the right side of the design facing outwards, position the acetate centrally over the aperture and stick in place.

Palm Beach

DIMENSIONS

Design: Length 14cm (5½in),
    width 11cm (4½in)
Whole card: 20cm (8in),
    width 15cm (6in)
Aperture: Length 10cm (4in),
    width 7cm (2⅜in)

MATERIALS

* ✳ Acetate: OHP photocopy transparency
    sheet, template
* ✳ 1 white double-fold greeting card with
    oblong aperture, shallow box
* ✳ Glue stick
* ✳ White spirit
* ✳ Real fine sand or gold glitter
* ✳ Real tiny shells
* ✳ Acetate (OHP) pen
* ✳ Clear varnish
* ✳ Paints: Pebeo Vitrail spirit-based – Emerald
    Green 13, Deep Blue 10, Turquoise Blue
    17, Brown 11. Lefranc & Bourgeois spirit-
    based – Cyan 087, Hiding White 004
* ✳ Paintbrush, scissors, masking tape

METHOD

1 Cut the sheet of acetate so that it is 15mm
(⅝in) larger on all edges than the card
aperture. Place the remaining acetate over the
palm tree and yacht templates and secure to a
flat surface with tape. Using the acetate pen,
trace the palm tree and yacht shapes on to the
acetate. Paint the palm tree leaves Emerald
Green and the tree trunk Brown. Paint the yacht
Emerald Green. Leave to dry for about 24 hours.

2 When dry, carefully cut out the palm tree
and yacht shapes. Place the oblong piece of
acetate over the background template and secure
to a flat surface with tape. Place a strip of masking
tape across the acetate below the top line shown

Tips
When you are cutting out the painted shapes,
it is advisable to hold the template or a piece
of paper over the painted surface. This will
prevent fingerprints from marking the surface.

If you are unable to obtain real sand, gold
glitter may be used for the beach.

on the template. Using the Deep Blue paint, paint the top section of the card. While wet, carefully peel off the masking tape. Place a second strip of masking tape across the acetate below the middle line shown on the template. Paint the section above this Turquoise Blue. This will blend gently into the edge of the Deep Blue, indicating the horizon. Using the end of the paintbrush draw waves in the wet Turquoise Blue paint. Carefully peel off the masking tape. Place a third strip of tape below the third line shown on the template. Paint above this Cyan. While it is still wet, peel off the tape and paint the lower section White, allowing it to blend gently with the Cyan. Sprinkle the White paint

with sand while it is wet, and place the sea shells in position as shown. Leave to dry for about 24 hours.

3 When it is completely dry, paint clear varnish on the palm tree and yacht and stick on the reverse side of the acetate. Place the palm tree at the edge of the beach as shown and the yacht on the horizon. This will give a silhouette effect on the right side of the design. Leave to dry.

4 When it is dry, apply glue to the inside edge of the aperture and, with the right side of the design facing outwards, position the acetate centrally over the aperture and stick in place.

Get Well Soon

Send your get-well message
to a relative or a friend with cheerful poppies,
a simple face or spray of spring flowers.
Whichever you send, you will be certain
to raise a smile.

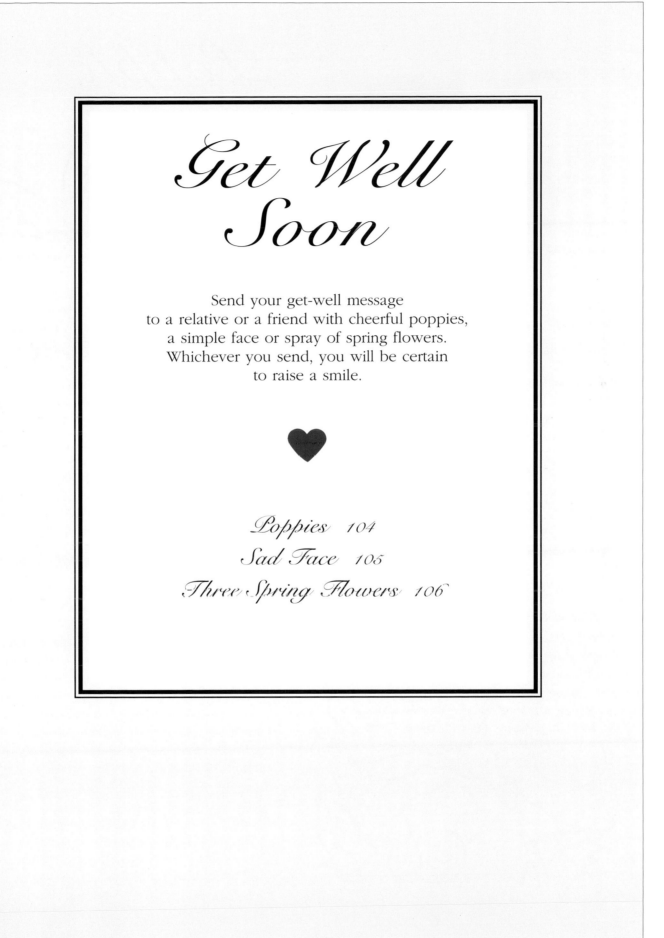

Poppies 104

Sad Face 105

Three Spring Flowers 106

Poppies

DIMENSIONS

Design: Length 10cm (4in),
    width 9cm (3¾in)
Whole card: Length 15cm (6in),
    width 10cm (4in)
Aperture: Length 8cm (3¼in),
    width 8cm (3¼in)

MATERIALS

* ✳ Acetate: OHP photocopy transparency
    sheet, template
* ✳ 1 white double-fold greeting card with
    square aperture, envelope
* ✳ Grey outliner
* ✳ Glue stick
* ✳ White spirit
* ✳ Paints: Pebeo Vitrail spirit-based –
    Crimson 12, Green Gold 22, Black 15
* ✳ Paintbrush, scissors, tape

METHOD

1 Cut the sheet of acetate so that it is 15mm
(⅝in) larger on all edges than the size of
the card aperture. Place the acetate over the
template and secure to a flat surface with tape.
Following the outline of the design, apply the
outliner to the acetate, making sure that there
are no gaps where they join. Leave to dry for
2 hours.

2 When the outliner is completely dry, paint
the poppies and leaves. Leave to dry for
about 24 hours. When the paint is dry, add a
few dots of outliner to the black centre of the
poppies and leave to dry for 2 hours.

3 Apply glue to the inside edge of the
aperture and, with the right side of the design
facing outwards, position the acetate centrally
over the aperture and stick down.

Tip

When you are applying outliner or paint
to a large design, such as these poppies, it is
best to work from the centre outwards.
This will prevent your hands or
fingers touching the wet surfaces.

Sad Face

DIMENSIONS

Design: Diameter 7cm (2¾in).
Whole card: Length 15cm (6in),
    width 10cm (4in).
Aperture: Length 8cm (3¼in),
    width 8cm (3¼in).

MATERIALS

* ✳ Acetate: OHP photocopy transparency
    sheet, template
* ✳ 1 white double-fold greeting card with
    square aperture, envelope
* ✳ Black outliner
* ✳ 2 shades of blue tapestry or knitting
    wool
* ✳ Needle and invisible thread
* ✳ Small round sticker
* ✳ Lazer white glitter
* ✳ Pebeo Vitrail clear varnish
* ✳ 1 small copper cow bell
* ✳ Paintbrush, scissors, barbecue skewer, spray
    starch, tape

METHOD

1 Place the sheet of acetate over the template
    and secure to a flat surface with tape.
Following the outline of the design, apply the
outliner to the acetate. Leave to dry for about 2
hours.

2 When the outliner is dry, paint the teardrop
    with clear varnish, and while this is still wet
sprinkle with white glitter. When completely dry,
carefully cut around the outer edge of the face,
cutting close to the outliner.

3 To make the wool curly for the hair, wrap
    the lengths of wool one at a time around a
skewer. Secure the ends with tape. Spray the
wool with starch and leave to dry completely.

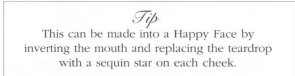

Tip
This can be made into a Happy Face by
inverting the mouth and replacing the teardrop
with a sequin star on each cheek.

When it is dry, remove from the skewer and you
should have a ringlet effect. Cut the wool into
short lengths.

4 Tie the cow bell in the middle of a length
    of invisible thread and, keeping the bell in
the centre, tie the wool together in the middle
with the thread. With the needle and remaining
ends of the thread, stitch the wool securely to
the top of the head and then secure the thread
on the inside top edge of the aperture with a
small sticker.

Three Spring Flowers

DIMENSIONS

Design: Length 7cm (2³/₄in),
   width 11cm (4¹/₂in),
Whole card: Length 10cm (4in),
   width 15cm (6in)
Aperture: Length 7cm (2³/₄in),
   width11cm (4¹/₂in)

MATERIALS

* ❉ Acetate: OHP photocopy transparency
     sheet, template
* ❉ 1 white double-fold greeting card with
     oblong aperture, envelope
* ❉ Grey outliner
* ❉ Glue stick
* ❉ White spirit
* ❉ Paints: Pebeo Vitrail spirit-based – Yellow
     14, Green Gold 22, Turquoise Blue 17,
     Deep Blue 10, Emerald, Rose Pink 21.
     Lefranc & Bourgeois spirit-based – Light
     Green 556, White 004
* ❉ Paintbrush, scissors, tape

METHOD

1 Cut the sheet of acetate 10mm (⁵/₈in) larger
   on all edges than the size of the card
aperture. Place the acetate over the template and
secure to a flat surface with tape. Beginning with
the flower on the left, follow the outline of the
design and lay the outliner on the acetate.
Complete one flower and stem at a time. Leave
to dry for about 2 hours.

2 When it is completely dry, begin again with
   the flower on the left and apply the paint to
the design. Leave to dry for 24 hours. When dry,
add several dots to the centre of the middle
flower using the outliner. Leave to dry for about
2 hours.

3 Apply glue to the inside edge of the aperture,
   and with the right side of the design facing
outwards, position the acetate centrally over the
aperture and stick in place.

It's Party Time

It's time to celebrate with a party.
Send your invitations with any one of these
superb party cards.
With bobbing balloons and psychedelic patterns,
or the perfect present they are fun to make,
a pleasure to send and great to receive.

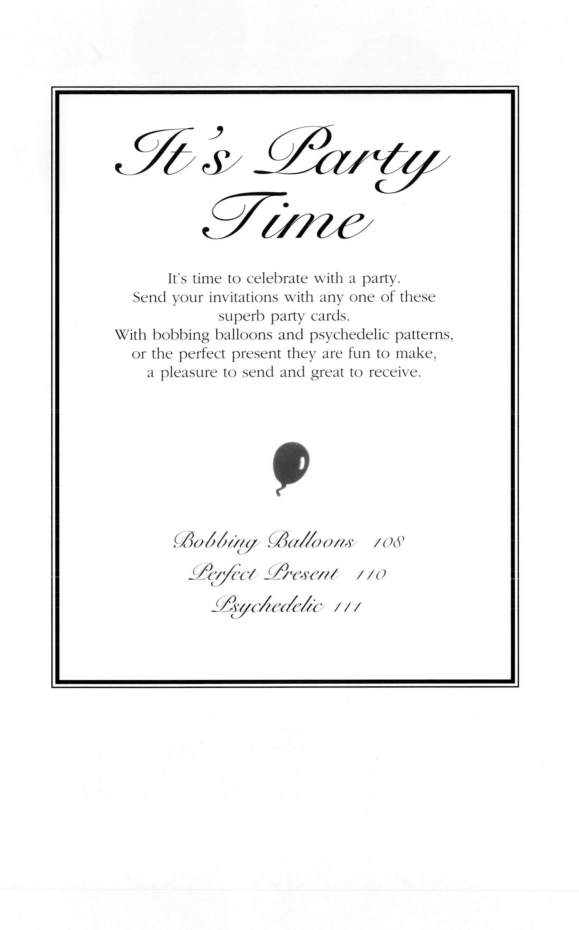

Bobbing Balloons 108

Perfect Present 110

Psychedelic 111

Bobbing Balloons

DIMENSIONS

'Party' Design: Length 9cm (3³⁄₄in),
 width 6cm (2¹⁄₂in)
Whole card: Length 15cm (6in),
 width 10cm (4in)
White card size: Length 12cm (4³⁄₄in),
 width 8cm (3¹⁄₄in)

MATERIALS

* ✳ Acetate: OHP photocopy transparency sheet, templates
* ✳ 1 orange double-fold greeting card, large envelope or shallow box
* ✳ White card
* ✳ Silver outliner
* ✳ Lazer silver glitter
* ✳ Assorted party sequins
* ✳ 28 gauge gold-coloured beading wire
* ✳ White spirit
* ✳ Glue stick
* ✳ 2 small round stickers
* ✳ 2 double-sided sticky pads

* Paints: Pebeo Vitrail spirit-based –
    Crimson 12, Yellow 14, Orange 16.
    Lefranc & Bourgeois spirit-based –
    Cyan 087, Purple 350, Light Green
    556. Pebeo Porcelain 150 water-based
    – Lapis Blue 16, Ruby 07, Saffron 03,
    Sapphire 18, Emerald 19
* Paintbrush, scissors, craft scissors, pinking
    shears, tweezers, craft pliers, tape

METHOD

1 Place the sheet of acetate over the 'Party'
template and secure to a flat surface with
tape. Following the outline of the letters, apply
the outliner to the acetate. While it is wet,
sprinkle with glitter. Shake off excess glitter.
Leave to dry for about 2 hours.

2 When it is dry, paint the letters as follows –
P: Sapphire, A: Ruby, R: Saffron, T: Lapis
Blue, Y: Emerald. Leave to dry for 48 hours. For
the six balloons paint acetate squares in the
colours Cyan, Purple, Light Green, Crimson,
Yellow and Orange. Leave to dry for about 24
hours.

3 Using shaped craft scissors or pinking
shears, cut out the white card to the size
indicated. Apply glue to the wrong side of the
card and stick centrally on to the front of the
orange greetings card.

4 When the painted letters are dry, carefully
cut around the word. When the painted
acetate squares are dry, place the balloon
template over the painted side – this will prevent
fingerprints marking the surface – and cut out
the acetate balloons. Using scissors, cut six
lengths of craft wire of various lengths. Twist one
end of each wire around the end of the balloons
using craft pliers. Join the remaining ends of wire
together by twisting them around each other.
Position the end of the wires in the centre of the
white card and secure in place with small stickers. Place the two double-sided sticky pads centrally on the card, one on each side of the wires.
Attach the word 'Party' to the pads.

5 To complete the card, use a glue stick and
tweezers to place party sequins around the
white card as shown on the design.

Perfect Present

DIMENSIONS

Design: Length 7cm (2³/₄in),
   width 7cm (2³/₄in)
Whole card: Length 14cm (5¹/₂in),
   width 14cm (5¹/₂in)
Aperture: 9cm (3³/₄in),
   width 9cm (3³/₄in)

MATERIALS

* ❋ Acetate: OHP photocopy transparency
   sheet, template
* ❋ 1 white double-fold greeting card
   with square aperture, envelope
* ❋ Gold outliner
* ❋ Lazer pale gold glitter
* ❋ Lazer crystal glitter
* ❋ Assorted gold, silver, clear, pink and
   purple sequins
* ❋ 1 gold-coloured cat bell
* ❋ Gold ribbon, shredded (optional)
* ❋ 1 small round sticker
* ❋ White spirit
* ❋ Glue stick
* ❋ Needle and invisible thread
* ❋ Gloss varnish
* ❋ Paints: Pebeo Porcelain 150 water-based
   – Fuchsia Pink 09, Parma 14
* ❋ Paintbrush, scissors, tweezers, craft knife,
   metal ruler, tape

METHOD

1 For the acetate border, cut a piece of acetate
12cm (4³/₄in) square. Use the craft knife and
ruler to cut out a square measuring 7cm (2³/₄in)
× 7cm (2³/₄in) from the centre of the sheet of
acetate. Place this piece of acetate over the
present template and secure to a flat surface
with tape. Following the outline of the design,
apply the outliner to the acetate. While it is still
wet, sprinkle with pale gold glitter. Shake off
the excess glitter. Leave to dry for about 2 hours.

2 When it is dry, paint the present Fuchsia Pink
and the ribbon bow Purple. While it is still
wet, use tweezers to place the hearts and stars
sequins on the present. Leave to dry for about 48
hours.

3 Paint the acetate border with the gloss varnish.
While it is wet, place the assorted sequins
around the inner edge of the border using the

tweezers. Sprinkle with crystal glitter and leave to dry for about 24 hours.

4 When the acetate border is dry, apply glue to the inside edge of the card aperture and, with the right side facing outwards, position the border centrally over the aperture and stick it in position.

5 When the present is completely dry, use the needle and a length of invisible thread to attach the bell to the centre of the bow. Position the remaining thread centrally on the top inside edge of the aperture of the card, and let the present hang centrally in the border. Secure the thread in place with a sticker.

Option
Shred the gold paper ribbon and curl it with scissors. Drape around the thread and allow to hang down over the present.

Psychedelic

DIMENSIONS
Design: Length 9cm (3³/₄in),
   width 7cm (2³/₄in)
Whole card: Length 11cm (4¹/₄in),
   width 9cm (3³/₄in)

MATERIALS
* Acetate: OHP photocopy transparency sheet, template
* 1 yellow double-fold greeting card

* Silver hologram card, envelope
* Silver outliner
* Lazer silver glitter
* Balloon and party sequins
* White spirit
* Glue stick
* Paints: Pebeo Vitrail spirit-based – Rose Pink 21, Yellow 14, Orange 16. Lefranc & Bourgeois spirit-based – Light Green 556, Cyan 087, Purple 350
* Paintbrush, pinking sheers, corner craft scissors, ruler, ball-point pen, tape

METHOD
1 Cut a piece of silver hologram card so that it is 15mm (⁵/₈in) larger than the design size. Mark the actual design size on the right side of the card. Match the template with the design size and lay the template over the hologram card and secure to a flat surface with tape. Using a ruler and ball-point pen, follow the lines of the design to leave an outline impression of the design on the hologram card. Remove the template.

2 Paint the diagonal sections marked on the card as follows – begin at the top right

hand corner with Orange, then Light Green, Yellow, Rose Pink, Cyan and Purple. While still wet, use the opposite end of the paint brush and make squiggles in the paint as shown. Leave to dry for 24 hours.

3 When the paint is completely dry, write the words 'Party Time' using the outliner. While the outliner is still wet, sprinkle with glitter. Shake off excess glitter. Leave to dry for about 2 hours.

4 When the paint is completely dry, use pinking shears to cut out the card along the lines marked for the design. Apply glue to the wrong side of the card and place it centrally to the front of the yellow greetings card and stick down. Using the corner craft scissors, cut four corners out of the remaining hologram card. Stick these to each corner of the painted card. Use tweezers and glue to stick party sequins and balloons to the surface of the design and along the two sides of the yellow card.

Tips

When you are cutting out the acetate, make sure you use a sharp blade in your craft knife, and a metal ruler. This will help you to cut clean straight lines and neat corners. Always cut on to a cutting mat or wooden cutting board.

Select and arrange your sequins on a plain piece of paper before you stick them down on the finished design.

Halloween

Hubble-bubble, toil and trouble
seeing the witch will make you wobble,
and the spider will make you scream.
Trick or treat the ghost you'll meet
who celebrates Halloween.

Witch 114

Spider 116

Ghost 118

Witch

DIMENSIONS

Design: Length 12cm (4¾in)
　　width 6cm (2½in)
Whole card: Length 20cm (8in),
　　width 15cm (6in)
Aperture: Length 14cm (5½in),
　　width 9cm (3¾in)

MATERIALS

* ❊ Acetate: OHP photocopy transparency
　　sheet, template
* ❊ 1 white double-fold greeting card with
　　oblong aperture, envelope
* ❊ Copper outliner
* ❊ Small silver stars and moon sequins
* ❊ Halloween sequins
* ❊ Wooden skewer for the broomstick
* ❊ Gold tassel
* ❊ Orange paper ribbon, shredded
* ❊ Small round stickers
* ❊ Glue gun or strong glue
* ❊ Glue stick
* ❊ White spirit
* ❊ Needle and invisible thread
* ❊ Paint: Pebeo Vitrail spirit-based –
　　Black 15
* ❊ Paintbrush, scissors, tweezers, tape

METHOD

1 Place the sheet of acetate over the template and secure to a flat surface with tape. Following the outline of the witch design, apply the outliner to the acetate. Leave to dry for about 2 hours.

2 When it is dry, paint the witch with Black paint. While still wet, use the tweezers to place a moon sequin on the witch's hat and star sequins as shown. Leave to dry for about 24 hours.

3 When the paint is completely dry, use the glue gun or strong glue to stick the wooden skewer to the centre of the reverse side of the witch. Glue the gold tassel to the lower end of the skewer.

4 Using a needle and a short length of invisible thread, attach the thread to the upper edge of the witch and secure with a knot. Position the end of the thread on the inside top edge of the aperture, allowing the witch to hang centrally. Secure the thread with a sticker.

5 To decorate, shred short lengths of orange paper ribbon and curl them over the blade of your scissors. Using small round stickers, attach the ribbons to the inside top edge of the aperture. Stick Halloween sequins around the border of the card.

Spider

DIMENSIONS

Design: Length 3cm (1¼in),
     width 7cm (2¾in)
Whole card: Length 15cm (6in),
     width 10cm (4in)
Aperture: Length 8cm (3¼in),
     width 8cm (3¼in)

MATERIALS

✳ Acetate: OHP photocopy transparency
     sheet, template
✳ 1 white double-fold greeting card with
     square aperture, envelope or shallow box
✳ Black outliner
✳ 2 small plastic eyes
✳ 1 black pipe cleaner
✳ Halloween sequins
✳ Narrow translucent ribbon
✳ Glue gun or strong glue
✳ Glue stick
✳ White spirit
✳ Small round sticker
✳ Short length of fishing line to make the
     spring, or invisible thread
✳ Paint: Pebeo Vitrail spirit-based – Black 15
✳ Paintbrush, scissors, tweezers, tape

METHOD

1 For the spider, cut a square of acetate
measuring approximately 7cm (2¾in).
Place this over the template and secure to a flat
surface with tape. Following the outline of the
spider, apply the outliner to the acetate. Leave to
dry for about 2 hours.

2 When it is dry, paint the the spider with
Black paint. While it is still wet, use tweezers
to place the plastic eyes 1cm (⅜in) apart. Leave
to dry for about 24 hours.

3 When the paint is completely dry, cut the
pipe cleaner to make two 11cm (4½in)
lengths. Use the glue gun or strong glue to stick
both pipe cleaners to each edge of the reverse
side of the spider shape. Bend the pipe cleaners
into position to form the spider's legs.

4 To make a spring to support the spider, cut
a length of fishing line and secure one end
to a wooden skewer. Wrap the line tightly
around the skewer for approximately 4cm
(1½in) leaving a straight length of line. Secure
this to the skewer. Warm the skewer under a
hairdryer for about 2 minutes. Leave to cool.
Remove the spring from the skewer and cut to
the required length, leaving the straight end for
attaching to the card. Using the glue stick or
strong glue, stick the end of the spring to the
reverse side of the spider, letting the spider
dangle from it.

5 Position the end of the spring on the inside
top edge of the aperture and secure in
place with a sticker. Cut 9cm (3½in) lengths of
translucent ribbon. Use the glue stick to fix
them along the inside top edge of the aperture,
allowing them to hang down behind the spider
to give a cobweb effect. Stick Halloween sequins
around the front of the card.

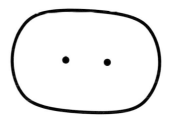

Tips

If you are unable to obtain fishing line for the
spring, you can hang the spider with a straight
length of invisible thread.

The strips of translucent ribbon can be stuck in
place using adhesive tape. Cut a length of tape long
enough to fit across the top of the aperture and,
with the sticky side upwards, lay the ends of the
ribbon on the tape. Then stick the tape to the
inside edge of the card above the aperture.

Ghost

DIMENSIONS
Design: Length 6cm (2½in),
    width 6cm (2½in)
Whole card: Length 11cm (4½in),
    width 9cm (3¾in)
Aperture: Length 6cm (2½in),
    width 6cm (2½in)

MATERIALS
* ❋ Acetate: OHP photocopy transparency
    sheet, template
* ❋ 1 black double-fold greeting card with
    square aperture, envelope
* ❋ Grey outliner
* ❋ Lazer silver glitter
* ❋ Small white sticker
* ❋ Strong glue
* ❋ White spirit
* ❋ Paint: Inscribe luminus acrylic Glow
    Paint
* ❋ Paintbrush, scissors, tape

METHOD

1 Place the sheet of acetate over the template and secure to a flat surface with tape. Following the outline of the design, apply the outliner to the acetate. While it is still wet, sprinkle with glitter. Shake off the excess. Leave to dry for about 2 hours.

2 When the outliner is dry, paint the ghost design with glow paint. Make sure that you paint right up to the outliner, leaving no gaps for the light to shine through. Leave to dry for about 24 hours.

3 When the paint is completely dry, carefully cut around the ghost shape. Cut a small oblong of clear acetate and use strong glue to attach it to the reverse side of the bottom edge of the ghost. Position the acetate to the inside bottom edge of the aperture and secure with a sticker. This piece of acetate will help the ghost to sway backwards and forwards.

Tip
When you are cutting out the painted ghost it is advisable to hold a piece of paper over the painted surface to prevent fingerprints from marking the surface.

Blank Cards for Any Occasion

A selection of designs which can be used for almost any occasion.

Blue Waves 120

Moon, Shooting Star and Planet 121

Sea Shells 122

Blue
Waves

DIMENSIONS

Design: Length 10cm (4in),
   width 9cm (3³⁄₄in)
Whole card: Length 15cm (6in),
   width 10cm (4in)
Aperture size: Length 8cm (3¹⁄₄in),
   width 8cm (3¹⁄₄in)

MATERIALS

* ✻ Acetate: OHP photocopy transparency sheet, template
* ✻ 1 white double-fold greeting card with square aperture, envelope
* ✻ Silver outliner
* ✻ Lazer white glitter
* ✻ Sequin fish confetti
* ✻ Glue stick
* ✻ White spirit
* ✻ Paints: Lefranc & Bourgeois spirit-based – Cyan 087. Pebeo Vitrail spirit-based – Turquoise Blue 17, Deep Blue 10. Pebeo Liquid Crystal water-based – Bright Blue 14.
* ✻ Paintbrush, scissors, tweezers, tape

METHOD

1 Cut the sheet of acetate so that it is 15mm (⁵⁄₈in) larger all round than the card aperture. Place the acetate centrally over the template and secure to a flat surface with tape. Following the outline of the design, apply the outliner to the acetate. Leave to dry for about 2 hours.

2 When the outliner is dry, paint the top section of the waves in Cyan, the second section in Bright Blue, the third section in Turquoise Blue and the lower section in Deep Blue. While the paint is still wet, use tweezers to place fish sequins between the bottom three sections, and sprinkle the tops of the waves with glitter. Leave to dry for about 24 hours.

3 When it is completely dry, apply glue to the inside edges of the card aperture and, with the right side of the design facing outwards, position the acetate centrally in the aperture and stick in position.

Moon, Shooting Star and Planet

DIMENSIONS

Design: Length 15cm (6in),
   width 4.5cm (1³/₄in)
Whole card: Length 18cm (7in),
   width 5cm (2in)
Aperture: Length 12cm (5in),
   width 3cm (1¹/₄in)

MATERIALS

* ❋ Acetate: OHP photocopy transparency
   sheet, template
* ❋ 1 white double-fold greeting card with
   oblong aperture, envelope
* ❋ Silver, gold and grey outliners
* ❋ Lazer silver and gold glitters
* ❋ Small silver and gold star sequins
* ❋ Glue stick
* ❋ White spirit
* ❋ Pebeo clear varnish
* ❋ Paints: Pebeo Vitrail spirit-based – Deep
   Blue 10, Yellow 14; Lefranc & Bourgeois
   spirit-based – Hiding White 004
* ❋ Paintbrush, scissors, tweezers, tape

METHOD

1 Cut the sheet of acetate so that it is 15mm (⁵/₈in) larger all round than the aperture of the card. Place the acetate over the template and secure to a flat surface with tape. Apply the outliners to the acetate, following the outline of the moon in silver outliner, the star in gold and the planet in grey. Leave to dry for about 2 hours.

2 When it is dry, paint clear varnish around the outer rim of the planet and the tail of the shooting star. While it is still wet, sprinkle silver glitter around the planet and gold glitter along the tail of the shooting star. Shake off the excess. Paint the moon and planet Hiding White, the star Yellow and the background Deep Blue. While it

is wet, sprinkle with crystal glitter, and use tweezers to place the silver and gold star sequins on to the paint as shown. Leave to dry for about 24 hours.

3 When the design is completely dry, apply glue to the inside edges of the card aperture. With the right side of the design facing outwards, position the acetate centrally over the aperture and stick in position.

Tip
A card with a gold border was chosen to highlight the shooting star design. Cards with silver borders are also available and this would complement the silver glitter used on this design

Sea Shells

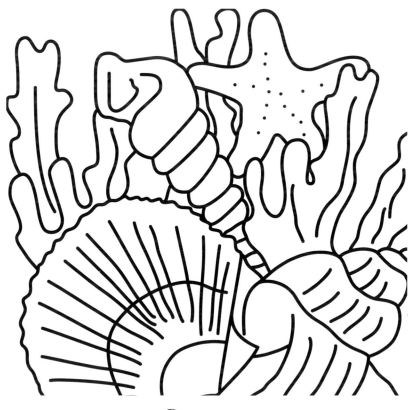

DIMENSIONS
Whole card: Length 20cm (8in), width 15cm (5¾in)
Aperture: Length 10cm (4in), width 10cm (4in)

MATERIALS

* ❊ Acetate: OHP photocopy transparency sheet, template
* ❊ 1 white double-fold greeting card with square aperture, envelope
* ❊ Grey outliner
* ❊ Lazer crystal glitter
* ❊ Clear sequin spots and small turquoise spots
* ❊ Tiny gold sequin stars
* ❊ Glue stick
* ❊ White spirit
* ❊ Paints: Lefranc & Bourgeois spirit-based – Hiding White 004, Purple 350. Pebeo Vitrail spirit-based – Yellow 14, Green Gold 22, Deep Blue 10, Rose Pink 21
* ❊ Paint brush, scissors, tweezers, tape.

METHOD

1 Cut the sheet of acetate so that it is 15mm (⅝in) larger all round than the card aperture. Place the acetate centrally over the design and secure to a flat surface with tape. Beginning at the top and following the outline of the design, apply the outliner to the acetate. Leave to dry for about 2 hours.

2 When the outliner is dry, paint the shells and starfish. While the paint is wet, sprinkle with the glitter and use tweezers to place the sequin stars in the centre of the starfish. Paint the seaweed and place clear and turquoise sequin spots onto the wet paint. Finally, paint the background Deep Blue. Leave to dry for about 24 hours.

3 When it is completely dry, apply glue to the inside edges of the card aperture and with the right side of the design facing outwards, position the acetate centrally over the aperture and stick in position.

> *Tip*
> Always clean paint brushes thoroughly with white spirit when using spirit-based paints and varnishes. Use clean water when you have been using water-based paints.

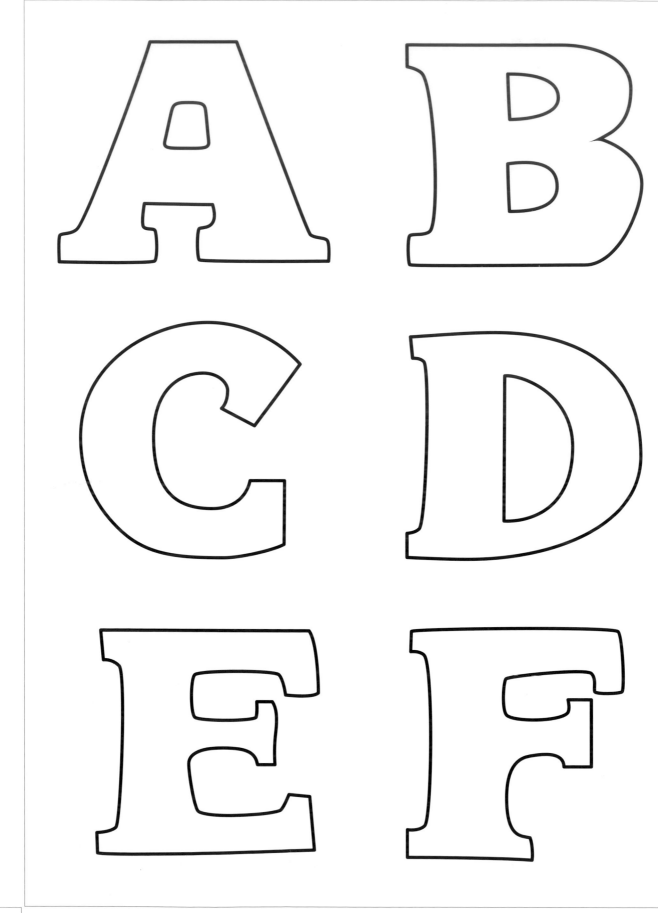

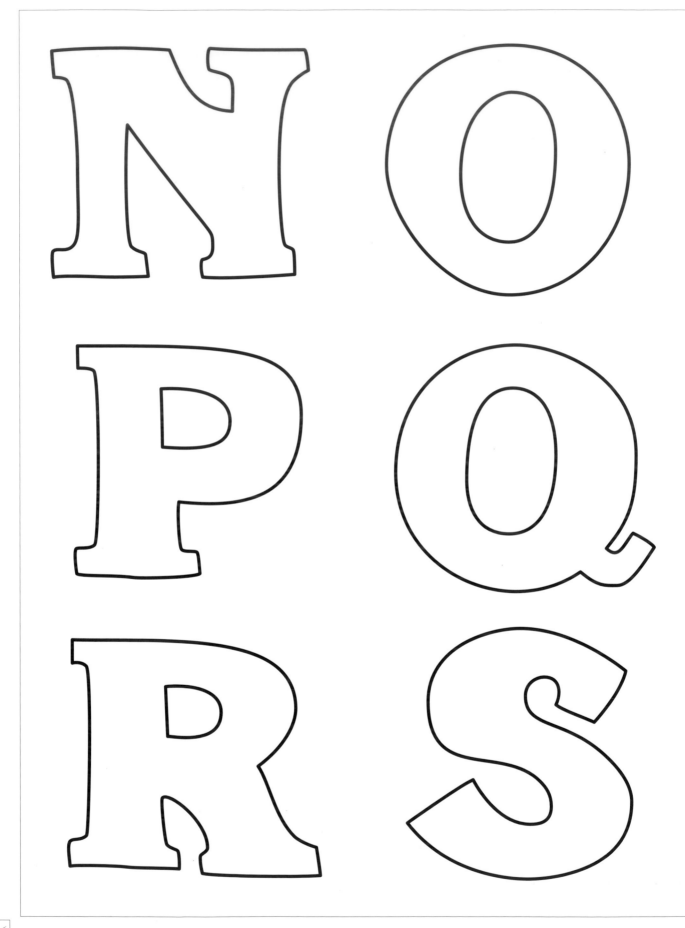

Suppliers

All the materials listed in the projects should be easily available from your local art and craft shop, stationer and department store. In case of difficulty, contact the following manufacturers for help.

PAINT AND OUTLINER

UK
Pebeo
Pebeo UK Ltd
109 Solent Business Centre
Millbrook Road West
Millbrook
Southampton SO15 0HW
Tel 01703 901914/5

Lefranc & Bourgeois
ColArt
Whitefriars Avenue
Harrow
Middlesex HA3 5RH
Tel 0181 427 4343

Talens Decorfin
Royal Sovereign Ltd
7 St Georges Industrial Estate
White Hart Lane
London N22 5QL
Tel 0181 888 3232

USA
Pebeo
Pebeo of America Inc
555 VT Route 78
Swanton
VT 05488
Tel 819 829 5012

Lefranc & Bourgeois
ColArt Americas Inc
11 Constitution Avenue
PO Box 1396
Piscataway
NJ 08855-1396
Tel 732 562 0770

Plaid Gallery Glass
Plaid Enterprises Inc
PO Box 2835
Norcross
GA 30091-2835
Tel 1 800 842 4197

Talens Decorfin
Canson-Talens Inc
21 Industrial Drive
South Hadley
MA 01075-0220
Tel 413 538 9250

Australia
Pebeo
Pebeo of Australia
Franchville
1-5 Perry Street
Collingwood
3066 Victoria
Tel 03 941 60611

Lefranc & Bourgeois
Jasco Pty Ltd
118-122 Bowden Street
Meadowbank
NSW 2114
Tel 02 980 71555

Talens Decorfin
Fine Art Products Pty Ltd
1st Marine Parade (PO Box 22)
Abbotsford
Victoria 3067
Tel 03 9415 9555

South Africa
Pebeo
Liserfarn Invest. Pty Ltd
PO Box 1721
Bedford View
Johannesburg 2008
Tel 011 455 6810

Lefranc & Bourgeois
Ashley & Radmore Pty Ltd
PO Box 57324
Springfield 2137
Johannesburg 2000
Tel 011 493 6509

Talens Decorfin
i'Kathi International cc
PO Box 422
Banbury 2164
Tel 011 795 3469

METALLIC CONFETTI

UK
Amscan International Ltd
Brudenell Drive
Brinklow
Milton Keynes
MK10 0DA
Tel 0800 581 535

USA
Amscan Inc
80 Grasslands Road
Elmsford
NY 10523
Tel 1 800 444 8887

Australia
Amscan Asia Pacific
31 Freeman Street
Campbellfield
Victoria 3061
Tel 03 9357 0724

JONES TONES LAZER GLITTER

UK
F W Bramwell Co
Unit 8B
Simonstone Business Park
Blackburn Road
Simonstone
Lancashire BB12 7NQ
Tel 01282 779811

USA
Jones Tones
33865 United Avenue
Pueblo
CO 81001
Tel 719 948 0048

Australia
Aurora Traders
306 Murray Street
Perth 6000
Tel 08 932 19873

New Zealand
Creative Promotions
11 Hokio Sands Road
PO Box 307
Levin
Tel 06 368 3124

South Africa
Rubber Stamp & Engraving Co
South & Desmond Street
Kramerville
Sandton
Tel 01126 21400